Riding &Racing Techniques

by the editors of *Bicycling*® magazine

Rodale Press, Emmaus, Pennsylvania

Printed in the United States of America on recycled paper, containing a high percentage of de-inked fiber.

Senior Editor, Ray Wolf
Edited by Larry McClung
Cover photograph by John Hamel
Cover design by Linda Jacopetti and Karen A. Schell
Book design by Linda Jacopetti

Library of Congress Cataloging in Publication Data
Main entry under title:

Riding and racing techniques.

    Cover title: Bicycling magazine's riding and racing techniques.
    1. Bicycle racing. 2. Cycling. I. Bicycling!
II. Title: Bicycling magazine's riding and racing techniques.
GV1049.R46   1985   796.6   85-2257
ISBN 0-87857-545-6 paperback

    4 6 8 10 9 7 5 3   paperback

Contents

Introduction

The bicycle is such a familiar vehicle to most of us that it is easy to take riding it for granted. After all, we were all children once, and children typically spend a lot of time on their bikes. But when it comes to learning proper technique, our childhood riding habits often get in the way.

As children we probably paid little attention to gear selection (many of us only rode single-speed or three-speed bikes), became accustomed to pedaling intermittently and with low rpm, and knew next to nothing about good form on the bike. In addition, we probably rode on the wrong side of the street much of the time, ignored stop signs and traffic signals, and never thought about wearing special gloves or shoes, much less a safety helmet.

Becoming a safe and proficient cyclist is thus not a natural by-product of growing up but the result of hard work, practice, and a willingness to accept advice from riders more experienced than ourselves. Unfortunately, many highly skilled riders lack the patience needed to work with novices to nurture them along until they become competent. Rare indeed is the beginner who can find an expert rider willing to go out with him on a five to ten mile jaunt to teach him the basics of good bike handling.

Most of the time, the novice is forced to join a bike club and participate in its organized rides. But if he goes out with a beginners group, he doesn't learn much. And if he goes out with a group of more advanced riders—those accustomed to riding 30 or 40 miles at a time and drafting off one another to conserve energy—he will quickly find himself struggling to keep up. In such a group, there will always be some riders eager to push a rapid pace, and the rest will want to keep up.

Actually, if you can endure the humiliation of being left behind your first few times out, riding with a group of moderately advanced cyclists can be a very effective learning process. As you ride, you can watch the experienced riders, see the type of cadence they maintain, observe how they handle their bikes going up and down hills and around corners. In this way, you will acquire general knowledge about riding technique as well as learning the peculiarities and the etiquette followed by the riders in this particular group.

An example of a fairly successful group learning situation exists here at *Bicycling* magazine. In 1982, several members of the *Bicycling* staff and some of their friends began meeting every Thursday after work for a low-key, enjoyable ride. After a few weeks, the Thursday night ride developed into a well-defined institution. We always rode the same 22-mile, mostly flat course. We always rode at a moderate speed, usually cruising at 18 to 20 mph. Most of the time we rode in a strict double paceline. Good individual form and tight group formation were the most highly prized ingredients of this weekly event.

For some riders, including competitive cyclists who regularly rode a much longer, faster workout every Wednesday, the Thursday night ride was an easy rest-day workout. These well-conditioned riders could sit at the front of the paceline the entire time if they so chose, spinning a 60-inch gear at 105 rpm to refresh their legs after the previous day's workout. For others, the Thursday night ride was anything but easy. Riders who were accustomed to, say, a 12 to 15 mph pace and who were not very good at drafting were tested to their limit. These riders had no choice but to draft closely to maintain the group's pace since they weren't strong enough to ride that fast without drafting. They learned the hard way to devote the mental concentration necessary to ride in good formation. Any short lapse in concentration would put them five or ten yards off the back— and ten yards grows to 1,000 very quickly.

Most double-paceline group rides are much too fast for the novice to have any hope, and this ride was a rare exception to the rule. In this case, the novices were motivated by being shown they could learn to ride half again as fast and ten times as smooth, mostly by replacing bad bike-handling habits with good ones. Because it was possible for new riders to keep up, and because the "senior" riders in the group offered cheerful but adamant coaching on form and paceline etiquette, the new riders improved with dramatic speed.

A number of riders who initially lacked both strength and form learned to substitute form for strength. After having the painful experience of being dropped, chasing, and finding the group waiting patiently several miles up the road, they learned to be tenacious wheelsuckers, never allowing even the one-second lapses in concentration that used to be their downfall. Some of the people in this category were accustomed to riding with a stronger, faster spouse, and they all commented that they took coaching much more gracefully on the group rides than they did from their spouses. They would resent it if their spouses dropped them, but if the group dropped them, they were more likely to say their own powers of concentration and/or riding technique were at fault.

Indeed, several specific riding situations showed the novices in our small pack that technique and timing often meant more than strength. For example, whenever the group reached a small hill, the better riders would naturally shift into the right gear, get out of the saddle, gently increase their effort, and crest the hill with almost no change in speed. A rider at the back of the group, caught in a too-high gear and too slow to react by shifting, would lose speed and get dropped. The same was true of riding a tight echelon formation in a crosswind or cornering crisply without letting a gap appear between one's front wheel and the rear wheel ahead.

These were not sightseeing rides; their focus was more serious. Everyone involved was either teaching or learning riding technique. Still, some of the newer riders eventually mastered the art of simultaneously riding in a paceline and looking at the scenery, and on every ride, we made sure that everyone enjoyed a few joking moments. Ours was a cordial, noncompetitive group, but the first priority was riding technique, since no rider can learn very much of it without devoting some rides to total concentration.

The *Bicycling* Thursday night rides have continued, though

they have lost some of the discipline and focus on learning good technique that existed in their first year. Nonetheless, veterans of the original group continue to attest to the value of this collective approach to the teaching and learning of cycling skills. We offer it as a model for those of you who would like to find a better way to improve your technique than merely riding alone or with one or two friends. Try organizing experienced and novice riders of your acquaintance into a teaching-learning group that meets regularly, and discover for yourself the value of this approach.

While there is no substitute for hands-on experience, you can still learn a lot about good riding technique from reading the chapters that follow. There is something here for everyone, from the beginner to the skilled rider. We start with the fundamentals of properly setting up your bike and positioning yourself on it. We go on to describe many basic skills that even experienced riders can usefully review from time to time, and we conclude by discussing more advanced riding techniques. Though some of these techniques are particularly useful to those interested in racing, recreational riders and tourists can certainly adapt them to their own uses. Our hope is that reading this book will make the time you spend in the saddle more constructive, safe, and enjoyable.

The Editors,
Bicycling magazine

Part One
Building a Foundation for Good Riding Technique

Basic Riding Techniques

Don't think just because this chapter is about *basic* riding techniques that you should skip over it. Even accomplished riders continually work on the most basic of riding skills. They don't allow themselves to be fooled by the apparent simplicity of the task. Wiping off your tires while riding or putting your foot in a toe clip may sound easy enough, yet many riders continually and unknowingly repeat mistakes that could cause accidents.

One-Handed Riding

There are innumerable occasions while cycling when it becomes necessary to ride with just one hand on the handlebars. For simple things like changing gears, there is rarely any problem or danger, although the sale of bikes with stem shifters indicates that many cyclists lack the confidence to perform even this maneuver. At the other end of the riding spectrum, the most competent bike handlers can practically shift in their sleep, but they may run into difficulty trying to grab some food or an extra water bottle while riding at 25 mph. It might also be dangerous to keep just one hand on the bars for a long time such as while eating a sandwich or a piece of fruit.

Here's why. The steering of a bike is very unstable with only one hand on the bars. Should another rider bump into you, or should you hit a rock or rough spot in the road, the one hand on the bar may act as an unstable lever and send you out of control. The handlebar stem is the pivot point on the lever, so the farther from the stem your hand is placed on the handlebars, the greater the leverage and the more unstable the bike.

The simple trick for both the novice rider and the racer is to hold the bars right next to the stem. If you are fortunate enough to have ever watched any track racing, you've observed the riders in the Madison (team race) make seemingly daring high-speed changes. The relaying rider holds his bars with just one hand right next to the stem as he slings his partner into the race with the other hand. This simple technique, holding the bar near the stem, will allow you more control over the bike and reduce the risk of an accident while riding one-handed.

No Hands

Occasionally there are times when it is necessary to ride without any hands on the bars. For example, you might need to zip up a windbreaker before a descent, unwrap a sandwich,

Photograph 1–1. A rider in the Madison team race steadies his bike with one hand as he prepares to sling his partner into the race.

or put on or take off your gloves. Obviously without any hands on the bars, you are not in full control of the bike if something unexpected should happen.

Although there is really no completely safe technique to riding no-handed, there are a few things you can do to make it safer. First, you must check to see whether your bike will ride in a straight line. If your headset is pitted, the bicycle's smooth steering will be impaired so that without stabilizing hands on the bars it will want to go its own way. You can check your headset by slowly turning the handlebars while holding the front wheel off the ground. If the steering "locks in" or is tighter at any point in the rotation, then the headset is pitted. You or your local bike shop mechanic will have to do some work to fix the problem.

If you have been in a crash, your frame may have been bent out of alignment, causing your steering to pull distinctly to one direction. That can make it difficult or even impossible to ride without a hand guiding the bars. Here again, have a competent mechanic check out the frame. Another mechanical problem that can make it difficult to ride no-handed is a wheel out of true. If you take both hands off the bars at high speeds, a bad wheel will cause the entire frame to wobble.

Once you've assured yourself that the bike is mechanically sound, you are ready to practice riding no-handed. If you have never ridden this way before, but feel steady enough to try it, here are a few suggestions. Sometime when you're out on a ride and well warmed up—say, a half hour or so into the ride—pick a smooth stretch of road with little traffic and get your bike moving at a moderately fast pace so you'll have some momentum to keep you steady. Stop pedaling and then try lifting your hands off the tops of the bars momentarily. Ride with your hands hovering at the bars until you find the steering predictable.

At this point, it should be apparent whether or not your bike is stable. If so, you should be able to sit back on the saddle and still have control of the bike. (Of course, there are no guarantees, so make sure you wear your helmet for this practice.) You'll find that you can guide the bike by shifting your weight from one side of the saddle to the other to make slight corrections. When you feel comfortable with this, try pedaling. Smooth pedaling and a good fitting bike are essential here. When you take both hands off the bars, always make certain that you can see sufficient road in front of you so you don't hit any potholes or rocks.

Looking Behind You

Turning to look behind you is not really a difficult maneuver. A little practice in any empty parking lot will assure that you can do this while continuing to ride a straight line. One important trick—when looking over your left shoulder—is to release your left hand while continuing to steer with your right arm. In this way, you can swivel your whole torso without inadvertently twisting the bars.

Another method for looking behind you, if you are in a tucked position on the drops of the handlebars, is to look under your arm. It's no way to go sightseeing, but we recommend this for racers who are a few seconds off the front of a chasing pack and cannot afford the precious time to sit up and look back. This is also a good technique for checking traffic to your rear when going down a steep hill.

Photograph 1–2. Notice the way this racer drops one arm to twist his body for a look behind.

Wiping Off Tires

If you wipe off your tires immediately after you run over some glass, you have a good chance of saving yourself a flat tire. There is a much better chance of brushing off the glass before it goes through the tread while you're still riding than if you brake to a stop and dismount before cleaning your tires. Brushing off the tires while on the move is quite simple and safe to do if you use the proper technique and wear gloves to protect your hands from glass cuts.

Wiping off the front tire is fairly basic. With the palm of your hand lightly touching the tire in front of the brake, brush for about two wheel revolutions. Make sure you keep your fingers away from the spokes. You might want to use the previously discussed method of riding one-handed for this.

Photograph 1–3. To wipe off your rear tire while riding, hook your thumb around a seatstay and slide the palm of your hand down until it meets the tire.

Wiping off the back tire is more dangerous. Riders have been known to crash or nearly lose a hand while trying to clean their rear tires. Generally what happens is that the rider, unable to see what he is doing, sticks his fingers in the spokes, or even worse, gets his hand caught between the seat tube and the moving tire. To avoid any danger of this, simply wrap your thumb around one of the rear seatstays and with your palm centered over the tire, slide your hand slowly down until it brushes the tire. Remember, using the padded palm of your glove will save you from the possibility of glass cuts.

Toe Clips

Have you ever seen (or been involved with) a rider crashing at the very start of a race, even before getting both feet in toe clips? What could be more basic for a cyclist than inserting feet into toe clips? If you already use clips and cleats, it should be easy for you to improve your technique.

If you're using toe clips and straps for the first time, be sure you familiarize yourself with the release mechanism; remember that your foot is removed by pulling it out to the back, not to the side. Before starting out, put one foot in the toe clip and tighten the strap. Raise that pedal into the up position so that you start the bike moving when you push down the pedal. Then before trying to insert your other foot, take five to ten pedal strokes, at least, so that you build up some momentum on the bike. This should eliminate any tendency to wobble when you stop pedaling to put the other foot in.

More experienced riders may still get fumble-itis in a racing situation. Sometimes, because of nervousness, getting the pedal, toe clip, and foot all lined up just right is difficult. There is a danger of crashing if you pay more attention to getting your foot into the clip than watching where you are going.

When this country's top competitive cyclists are at the Olympic Training Center in Colorado Springs, the coaches insist that all road riders put one foot down whenever they stop for a red light. This forces them to regularly practice putting their

Photograph 1–4. Getting your feet in and out of toe clips smoothly is an important skill to develop, especially at the start of a race.

feet into toe clips. Simple practice like this can help you, too. Remember to keep looking ahead while you flip the clip into position with your toe and then slide your foot in. If after a couple of tries you still can't get your foot in, just reach down with your hand and put it in, all the while looking forward and not at the pedals. In a race, don't forget to take those five to ten pedal strokes with one foot out before trying to get into the toe clip. This way you will already have some speed built up and can't be left behind by the pack, and you won't be wobbly.

The riding techniques discussed in this chapter may not seem as exciting or important as learning to ride at breakneck speeds down hills and around corners. They are nonetheless useful and well worth practicing. Mastering basic techniques such as these will add to your overall ability as a bikehandler and may save you from unnecessary accidents, so learn them well now, then brush up on them again at the start of each new cycling season.

Championship Form

Becoming a good cyclist involves more than merely riding lots of miles and building up strength and endurance. At the outset, you need to make sure that you and your bike fit each other. Your bike needs to be set up properly so that you can ride it in the most efficient way.

Riding with bad form not only is a tremendous waste of energy, it invites problems such as strained muscles, tendons, and ligaments. If you want to ride like a champion, the best way to begin is by learning championship form. To some degree this will have to be accomplished through trial and error, but here are some basic pointers to set you in the right direction.

Saddle Height

Look at the right leg of the cyclist in photograph 1–5. Even though his pedal is at the bottom of the stroke, his knee is still bent. He doesn't have the saddle high enough to straighten his legs. Surprised? Don't be. This cyclist is doing the right thing. Most other cyclists have their saddles an inch or two too high. How can that be, when it feels so comfortable to ride a bike with a high saddle?

A saddle that's too high feels good to pedestrian muscles. It lets you ride the way you walk, but that's bad for cycling muscles. You'll never get the spin and snap to be a good cyclist with a saddle that's too high. Your saddle should be at a height where you can put your heels on the pedals and backpedal without having to rock your fanny side to side. Try it. If you flunk the test, lower your saddle. It will feel worse when you first get on the bike, but after a few rides, you'll find you prefer it.

As with all rules, there may be exceptions. If, for example, your feet are long in proportion to your legs, you may be able to raise your saddle a few millimeters higher than you otherwise should. This will be true in particular if you tend to pedal with your toes pointed slightly down rather than held even or raised a bit above your heels. Saddle height is one of the few adjust-

13

Photograph 1–5. The saddle should be set at a height that allows the knee to remain slightly bent at the bottom of a pedal stroke.

ments you can make easily and without spending any money, so take advantage of that fact to get it perfect!

Saddle Tilt

Ever notice how many casual cyclists have their saddles tilted down? Now look at the bikes of experienced, well-coached cyclists. Their saddles are level or even pointing slightly up. Having a saddle that tilts down is a common mistake, and it goes hand in hand with having your saddle too high. If your saddle is too high, it's painful to have it level. It will exert too much pressure on your crotch, and pressure on the nerves in the crotch can produce prolonged numbness, as many cyclists have learned through experience.

What's wrong with a saddle that tilts down? It pushes you into the handlebars. You have to fight to stay on the seat. As a result, your arms, shoulders, and hands do unnecessary work and get tired. When your seat is the proper height, you'll probably like it level, and you may find you are more comfortable with the nose pointed slightly up. That helps keep your weight off your hands, so your upper body remains relaxed during long rides.

Saddle Fore-And-Aft Position

There are several competing theories on what your fore-and-aft position should be. You'll have to decide between our two favorites.

In the best of all worlds, you don't adjust the saddle to affect the saddle-to-handlebar distance. Instead, you adjust the saddle to achieve the ideal relationship between it and the pedals. Then you get the proper length handlebar stem to make your upper body comfortable. What is the proper saddle-to-pedal relationship? One classic approach says the saddle should be set back for touring and comfortable riding and forward for racing and for cyclists who like to sprint and spin.

Another approach more in vogue these days is a uniform formula for all cyclists. It's designed to adjust the bike to suit your thigh length. Adjust the seat so that when the crank is at three o'clock, you could drop a plumb bob from the base of your *tibial tuberosity,* and it will come very close to the pedal spindle. Find your tibial tuberosity by extending your leg straight and feeling for the bony knob that is just below your kneecap. If you can't locate it, then drop the plumb bob from the bottom of your kneecap.

Plenty of other "one size fits all" formulas, each with its own faults, have been published at various times. Certainly there's no harm in experimenting with this adjustment. Try to ignore the change in upper body position when you evaluate the way different positions feel. Right now, leg position is the object of concern; the upper body will be dealt with later.

Toe Clip Length

The classic rule of thumb is that toe clips should position your foot so the ball is over the pedal spindle. It's a good rule, since at that point your foot is able to exert full leverage on the pedal, and you don't stress the weaker bones and joints in your toes. The exception to this rule applies to track specialists. Many of them like to move their feet back slightly on the pedals in order to make more use of their calf muscles. But if you use that position for all-around riding or for climbing, you may find yourself developing a sore Achilles tendon. If you try this modified toe clip position and find soreness becoming a problem, move your foot slightly forward again and that should remedy it.

If your toe clips are too small, you'll probably know it. You'll feel as if you aren't firmly planted on the pedal, and you won't be able to apply full power. Clips that are too small can be a source of unwanted strain, also. Toe clips that are too long are harder to detect, but you'll be starting to pedal on your arch—a bad habit. Again, you won't be able to apply full power. Many bikes come with toe clips too large for the people that buy them. Between that fact and the fact that oversize toe clips are more comfortable than undersize toe clips, there is a tendency for people to use toe clips that are too large.

Cleat Placement

Cleats, like toe clips, are supposed to keep the balls of your feet right over the pedal spindle. In addition, they lock the foot into a single sideways rotation position. The important thing here is to allow your feet to rotate naturally—inward, outward, or straight ahead, as your anatomy dictates. Keep in mind the fact that most people are not completely symmetrical, so if one of your feet toes in or out more than the other, don't worry.

The classic way to determine cleat position is to ride without cleats long enough to leave marks on the shoe and use those marks to guide cleat placement. Another way is to sit on the bike and have a friend draw a line on the shoe sole where it meets the rear pedal cage. Both these methods depend on your having proper toe clip size.

Crankarm Length

Most cyclists are reasonably well served by the standard 170-millimeter cranks found on the majority of adult bikes. But if you're very tall or very short, or if you have a distinctive pedaling style, you might benefit from longer or shorter cranks. The only shorter cranks commonly available are 165 millimeter. Five millimeters (about a quarter inch) might not seem like a lot, but you feel it twice—at the top and at the bottom of your pedal stroke. During the thousands of times you spin those cranks, it adds up to a noticeable difference. Cyclists desiring longer cranks have more choice: 172.5-, 175-, and 180-millimeter cranks are all easy to find.

For riders who feel they need some sort of guideline, William Farrell suggests you have someone measure your inseam from floor to crotch as you stand barefoot. (Farrell is the director of the New England Cycling Academy and creator of the Fit Kit—a collection of instructions, tools, devices, and tables for measuring a rider and determining the proper dimensions of a frame and components to match that person.) Here's Farrell's rule of thumb.

Inseam	Crank Length
29½ inches or less	less than 170 millimeters
29½ to 33 inches	170 millimeters
33 to 36 inches	172.5 millimeters
36 inches plus	175 millimeters

Farrell considers this guideline to be most useful to novices who feel they need some place to begin in determining an appropriate crank length, and he feels that it is workable for the types of riding that most people do. He is quick to point out that specialists will have their own preferences for cranks that may differ from this. If you pedal slowly, turning over tall gears, long cranks will give you more leverage with which to turn them over. If you like to spin, you can turn a shorter crank over more quickly.

Changing cranks is expensive, and you won't want to bother unless you're very dissatisfied with your current cranks, or you're building your own custom bike. A new set of crankarms can cost about $100, depending on the brand. Even so, it might be worth it if your height and leg length make you a misfit on standard length cranks.

Brake Lever Placement

Do not make major changes in brake lever placement unless you are a cyclist with very short arms. There are many safety hazards associated with locating brake levers far down on the drops or up on the tops of the handlebars. But, there is about an inch or so of allowable variation, and noticeable differences in riding style and comfort can be found within that inch.

Touring cyclists generally like their brakes a bit higher on the handlebars. That way, they can ride with their hands resting on the brake hoods in a near upright position. It's a comfortable posture for long rides. Racers like their brakes lower. This makes them bent over in a more aerodynamic position both when they have their hands resting on the hoods and when they're using the brakes. The choice is yours. Changing your brake position is a lot of work, but you can cheat and get the same effect by loosening the handlebar stem binder bolt and rotating the bars in the stem.

Handlebar Stem Length and Height

Handlebar stem height is easy to determine. Start out with the bars about an inch below your saddle. Then adjust them for comfort and for your riding style—lower for racing, higher for touring. (Many cyclists pick smaller frames for racing and larger frames for touring because of the effect frame size has on stem height adjustment.) Your stem length should put the bars in a comfortable position so that you can lean gently on the bars or take your weight off them as you please. If you're reaching too far forward to grab them, you'll have to lean on them the whole time. If they're too close to you, you'll feel cramped.

Two rules of thumb can guide you toward a sensible stem length. The better of the two is that your nose should be about an inch behind the handlebars when your hands are on the drops. A friend with a plumb line can measure this. The other rule is that as you ride with your hands on the brake hoods, the bars should hide the front hub from your view.

Warning: it's neither easy nor cheap to change your stem length. You don't want to buy a bunch of stems before you decide which length you prefer. See if your local cycling club or bike shop has an adjustable-length stem (made by Cinelli or TTT). You can borrow one and use it on the bike to find what length suits you best. If no adjustable-length stem is available, you might be able to experiment by trading stems and handlebars with friends. You should also be aware that not all stems properly fit into all frames, and many stems fit only their own brand of handlebars. Check with your dealer before you try to force-fit something that won't go.

As we said in the beginning, you may have to go through some trial and error before you get all the components on your bike set up just right. Once you do, however, the payoff will

Photograph 1–6. Racers generally set their handlebars a little lower than their saddles so they can ride in a low, aerodynamic position.

make the effort worthwhile. Your riding will be smoother, less stressful on your body, and more energy efficient. You can then make the best possible use of the various riding techniques described in this book.

Riding the Paceline

One of the most honorable traditions in bicycling is co-operation in maintaining the paceline. Riders rotate positions in a line, each one taking a turn at the front where he or she "pulls" the other riders into the wind for a while before swinging off and letting the next rider take the lead.

Though riding paceline is an important technique in long road races, it need not be limited strictly to racing situations. In Europe, it is not uncommon to see large groups of cycle-tourists, young and old, riding tight, fast echelons. Unfortunately, in this country most recreational riders—and many racers—don't know how to ride a paceline properly. There are four basic types of paceline riding formations. Each one has its own practical application.

Straight or Single Paceline

This is the most basic paceline formation; all the others are variations of it. Simply stated, the single paceline is one straight line of riders, each drafting closely behind the next. The rider at the front "breaks the wind" for a time and then eases off to the side and "soft pedals" until he can swing in at the back of the line, as shown in illustration 1–1.

For the majority of training, racing, and touring situations, this is the most efficient way to travel in groups of two or more riders. With skilled racers, as many as 15 riders may use a single

Photograph 1–7. Paceline riding is an important skill for road racers and long-distance group touring.

paceline effectively. For cyclists new to the technique, four riders make a good-size learning group. In races, breakaway groups almost always use this straight paceline. It is also the safest paceline for tourists to use when riding where there is traffic.

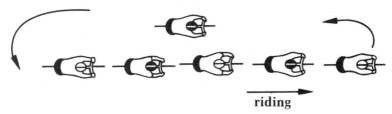

riding

Illustration 1–1. A single paceline formation.

Double Paceline

The best way to socialize on the bike is to ride in a double paceline. Riding two abreast, cyclists can carry on a conversation, talk shop, or whatever. This riding formation works the same as the single line. When the two riders have finished their turn at the front, they pull off, one to the right, the other to the left, and swing back alongside each other at the end of the line, as shown in illustration 1–2.

Cyclists at the Olympic Training Center log a majority of their early season miles riding in tight double paceline formations in groups of up to 24 racers. This not only provides companionship; it is also good practice for racing, since in a double paceline you simultaneously work on drafting closely behind someone and riding elbow to elbow with the rider next to you. However, before touring or training two abreast you should familiarize yourself with your local traffic laws, as this type of riding might not be legal.

If it is permissible to ride two abreast, make sure you drop back into the line quickly after taking your pull at the front. Motorists definitely don't like to see people riding four abreast. Racer Thomas Prehn reports that he was once stopped by the police before the Coors Classic in Colorado while training with the Swiss team. They were riding a double paceline, and when the officer saw them they were four abreast. The Swiss didn't understand English; the policeman didn't understand pacelines. Tom kept his mouth shut, and the group was allowed to continue their ride.

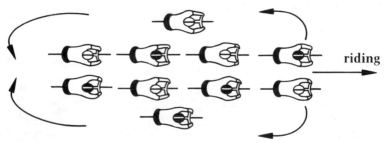

riding

Illustration 1–2. A double paceline formation.

Circular Paceline

The circular paceline is a bit more difficult, requiring more skill in controlling and handling your bike than either the single or double paceline. The formation begins with a single paceline, but as riders begin to swing off to one side it begins to resemble a double paceline. It differs from the double in that the two lines are moving at different speeds, the entire group moving constantly in a circular fashion—accelerating forward up the fast line and decelerating back along the slower line as shown in illustration 1–3.

This formation is best applied when there is a strong wind, and it's too tiring to stay on the front for a long pull. It also works well for large groups in a hurry. Each rider remains in front only briefly before swinging off in the direction established at the beginning, creating a steady succession of riders easing up on their pedals while waiting for the opportunity to swing back over to the rear of the primary line. When the time comes to rejoin the main line, a rider must quickly accelerate back to the speed of the person whose wheel he picks up. As you may well imagine, it takes a lot of concentration to ride this paceline properly. All of the riders in the group must be able to ride steadily and smoothly. Just one rider out of synch can throw the whole group off and ruin the effectiveness of the formation.

To ride a circular paceline properly, the cyclist on the front should spend only a few seconds pulling before swinging off—no more than about 15 pedal revolutions. The critical points in the circular paceline are when you swing off and decelerate and when you reaccelerate at the back. After riding this way and getting some experience at it, you will find it is best—after taking your "pull"—to start to ease off the front while you overlap the slower rider on your left by about a quarter of a wheel. By the time you are actually in position, enough space will have opened up so that he will be safely behind you. And at the back of the line, start to reaccelerate as the leading edge of your front wheel is about parallel to the bottom bracket of the rider next to you. With these techniques, the transitions from faster to slower and slower to faster lanes will be made more smoothly and efficiently.

Photograph 1–8. Team pursuit racers must learn to ride in very tight paceline formation to maximize their speed.

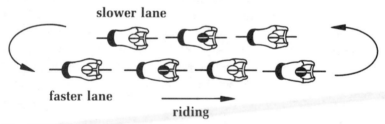

Illustration 1–3. A circular paceline formation.

Echelon or Crosswind Paceline

This is the hardest, most dangerous, but most enjoyable paceline to ride. The echelon (technically speaking, all pacelines are echelons) is a circular paceline adapted for crosswinds. Instead of lining up one rider behind the other, each cyclist is staggered off the rear flank of the one ahead, in order to stay protected from the wind. The rider on the front pulls off into the direction of the wind (for example, the right). He drops back until his front wheel has cleared the rear wheel of the next guy taking his pull. The cyclist in the decelerating lane then drops into the draft of the rider pulling just as he is beginning to drop back. When the cyclist reaches the last position of the slower lane, he then reaccelerates forward and into the slipstream of the rider ahead, as shown in illustration 1–4.

The echelon is, in all senses, a racing situation. You move diagonally forward and back, riders situated tightly off your handlebar and hip, with the riders directly in front moving in a different direction, at a different speed. As you can see, all of this takes a good deal of timing, coordination, and expert bike handling. With a group of riders that know how to ride in a crosswind properly this can really be a lot of fun ... at least as much fun as is possible to have with a stiff crosswind. Of course, when riders don't know what they are doing, an echelon will quickly turn into chaos.

Words of Caution—Paceline Etiquette

Any time you ride in a group you need to observe a few safety precautions. One of the most important is to never make any sudden moves, steering or braking. When cyclists are riding

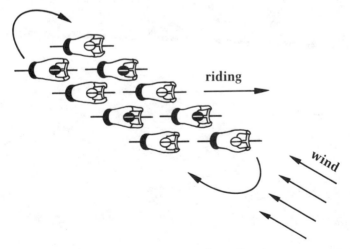

riding

wind

Illustration 1–4. An echelon formation for riding into a crosswind.

only a few inches apart, a sudden move by one will certainly cause an accident. If there is some danger ahead, try to brake steadily so everyone in the paceline can react. Also, try to steer gradually away from obstacles in the road rather than swerving at the last second.

Remember not to overlap wheels with the rider ahead or behind you. If he or she makes a sharp sideways movement into your wheel, you will almost surely go down. Riding slightly to the left or right of the wheel in front of you is a good idea, since it gives you a way out should that rider suddenly hit the brakes. Just make sure you also keep your wheel slightly behind his.

Photograph 1–9. Touring cyclists can also conserve time and energy by riding in pacelines.

On hills, many riders like to get out of the saddle for better leverage. When you do, you often move your body weight forward on the bike and "push" your bike back about six inches. The rider behind you has to stay alert for this so he doesn't overlap your rear wheel. (Many riders automatically get out of the saddle when they see the rider ahead of them do so.) Don't make your backward movement even worse by easing off the pedals and losing momentum when you get out of the saddle. You can lessen or even eliminate this tendency to bob back by getting out of the saddle as you enter a power stroke on the pedals. Push harder on the pedal to keep the bike's movement constant, and rise out of the saddle slowly and smoothly. Don't jump out.

Undoubtedly, when you first try it, riding paceline will seem exceedingly difficult. You will be tense, constantly afraid of making a mistake that will lead to a crash, but as you become more experienced, your skill and confidence will increase to the point that what once seemed daring and dangerous will become second nature. Eventually, you will not even have to watch the wheel you are following. You will develop instincts and know how close you are by watching the hips and saddle of the rider in front of you. At that point, you can relax and truly appreciate the joys and benefits of close riding in a group.

Part Two
Coping with Traffic and Road Hazards

Reading the Road

Plunging down a long hill one summer, cyclist Thom Lieb became aware that he was deep in a daydream, yet he was threading his bike through a maze of potholes and other hazards at almost 40 miles an hour. Thom says he has had the sensation of "automatic riding" before but never on such demanding terrain. He was amazed at the enormous amount of information that his senses were taking in and sorting out—without his conscious awareness.

Suddenly realizing you have been executing a difficult task unconsciously is always a bit of a shock, yet such incidents are not uncommon. Anyone who has ever driven long distances or typed a term paper has likely had an experience of this type. After a fumbling start, you eventually reach a point where you are working automatically. Your conscious mind is disengaged from the task, and you perform with utmost efficiency. The next thing you know, you're muttering, "Boy, those last 50 miles went fast," or "I really zipped through those ten pages."

You can never shift into automatic, though, unless you are first familiar with what you are doing. You can't expect to type ten pages an hour if you don't know the typewriter keyboard; likewise, you'll never be able to cycle automatically and with utmost safety and efficiency until you've first learned how to read the road. Basically, this is a two-part operation: first, you learn to spot obstacles, then you learn to take appropriate action. At the simplest level, every time you dodge a pothole, you are reading the road.

But even dodging a pothole may not be so simple. Potholes are usually obvious, but can just as easily be hidden. Shadows do a great job of camouflaging potholes. If the entire road is shadowed, your eyes will quickly adjust and spot the potholes and other hazards. But if the road is dappled with shadows, such as when the sun is shining through tree branches, it's almost impossible to tell which dark spots are safe to ride through and which aren't.

It's also hard to spot potholes when they're filled with water. What seems to be an innocent little puddle may be a wheel breaker in disguise. To avoid that possibility, treat dark and wet spots suspiciously. Skirt around them when you can, ride through them cautiously when you can't. Even when you can easily see a pothole, you often have little room to maneuver around it.

Quick Turn Maneuvers

Sometimes you can dodge a pothole with a quick weave. Flick your handlebars to one side, putting your bike into a lean for turning the opposite way. Then turn your handlebars back in the opposite direction to recover your original line, as shown in illustration 2–1. When you become good at this maneuver, you can make your bike lean first to one side, then to the other underneath you while you continue to ride nearly in a straight line. This way, you can avoid potholes without swerving into traffic.

A similar S-curve maneuver can be used to ride between two rocks or potholes that are side by side but at an angle to

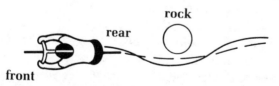

Illustration 2–1. A single obstacle such as a rock or pothole can be avoided with a quick weaving maneuver.

your path. Start your curve in the direction that will give you a line between the obstacles, as shown in illustration 2–2. Occasionally, though, you simply won't be able to avoid potholes since, on some roads, there are more potholes than pavement. When the holes are shallow, you can ride through them safely if you take your weight off the wheels. Get up off the saddle, and put your weight on the pedals and handlebars. If the holes are too deep to safely negotiate this way, look for a better road.

Be prepared to encounter potholes in the most unlikely of places, such as hidden behind a sharp rise in the pavement. Pavement ridges not only hide potholes, they also pose many other problems for cyclists. You'll usually find ridges where sections of the road have been repaved or where a shoulder has been added after the road was built. Usually the ridges are beveled so you can roll right up and down. But when there is no bevel, running into a ridge is just like riding into an inch-high wall; the impact can knock your wheels out from under you.

Bricks and stones can break your bones, too, if you're not careful. A stone jutting from the surface of a brick or cobblestone road can quickly drop you in your tracks. Use caution. Railroad and streetcar tracks can cut your journey short, as well. If your wheels slip into the tracks, you'll lose control of your bike and will quickly tumble to the ground. Try to cross tracks at as close to a right angle as possible. If you live in the West, you should also watch out for cattle guards. These consist of a group of railroad rails or steel pipes spaced three to six inches apart over a pit. They keep cattle from crossing the road, and can also gobble up a bicycle wheel if you approach at the wrong angle.

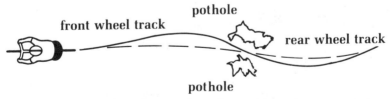

Illustration 2–2. A pair of obstacles side by side and at an angle to your path can be avoided by leaning your bike into a curve that will carry you cleanly between them.

Sewer gratings and bridge expansion joints can also snatch your wheels. Many communities have replaced the most dangerous type of grating, which runs parallel to the roadway, with safer ones that run at a diagonal or are cross-hatched. If you can't avoid riding over a grating, pass over the bars at as close to a right angle as you can. Of course, in most cases, simply being in the proper position on the road—at least three or four feet away from the curb or parked cars—will allow you to completely avoid this hazard. You usually can't cross a bridge expansion joint at a right angle; to do so, you'd have to ride across the path of traffic. But you should check each joint carefully and be prepared to dismount if the opening is big enough to swallow a wheel.

Other Hazards of the Road

There are plenty of other hazards that can send you sprawling to the ground if you aren't careful. Gravel is one of them. It's not hard to maneuver through a layer of fine gravel on top of a paved road, but when the entire road surface is gravel, riding becomes trickier. You can negotiate your way through finely crushed gravel by keeping your speed down and "paddling" with one foot to stabilize yourself, but it's virtually impossible to ride through larger chunks of gravel. Gravel is most dangerous in turns, where your traction is already low. Bumps, oil, and water also are often found in turns, and they all can dangerously reduce your traction.

Even excluding turns, oil and water can be hazardous. Water can make manhole covers, leaves, and lane markers as slippery as ice, and in winter, ice on the road is the major hazard. Oil collects at spots where cars wait for traffic lights and stop signs. About the worst condition you're likely to encounter is the mixture of oil and water that occurs shortly after the start of a rainstorm. During the first half hour of a storm, the rain mixes with the oil and grime on the road and forms a slippery solution that can cut the friction between your tires and the road to half of what it would be on a dry surface.

This loss of friction reduces your steering and braking control, causing you to skid if you brake too vigorously or to spill if you take a turn too quickly. To make matters worse, caliper brakes lose up to 95 percent of their effectiveness when they become wet. After the first half hour of a storm, most of the road grime and oil is washed away. Your traction rises to three-quarters of what it would be on a dry surface, but you still need about twice the distance to stop. At 16 mph, you need about 65 feet to stop; racing down a hill at 50 mph, you need about 500 feet, a full tenth of a mile.

Emergency Braking

The most important emergency braking maneuver is the panic stop. To stop short, you must apply the front brake forcefully since it has twice the stopping power of the rear brake. But you must be careful because the front wheel can lock during

Photograph 2–1. To make an emergency stop, shift your weight back on the bicycle while applying the front brake forcefully. Lighter pressure should be applied on the rear brake to avoid skidding.

a panic stop, throwing you over the handlebars. The correct technique for a panic stop eliminates this danger. Apply the rear brake *lightly* as you increase pressure on the front brake. Slide back on the saddle to increase weight on the rear wheel. When the rear wheel begins to skid, you know that it is close to lifting off, so you reduce pressure on the *front* brake.

It is important not to apply the rear brake too hard in a panic stop. Your stopping power is all in the front brake, especially since applying it shifts weight to the front wheel. Using the rear brake hard will only make the rear wheel skid sooner. You'll wear out your rear tire and not get any more stopping power. When you use the rear brake gently, the behavior of the rear wheel becomes a gauge that you can use to tell how hard you can squeeze the front brake.

Practice the panic stop technique and also practice to develop your reflex in case the bike starts to go out of control. This reflex must always be to *release* the brakes to restore traction. At a very low speed—two to three miles per hour— practice hitting the front brake harder and harder until the rear wheel actually lifts off the ground. As soon as it does, release the brake lever. Once you have developed the correct reflex, you have a fighting chance to keep control if you misjudge braking at normal speed.

For moderate stops when going straight on dry pavement, use the front brake alone. Then you can't skid, and you have one hand free for signaling or shifting gears. But to control speed downhill, use both brakes equally to divide the heat buildup. Of course, for any of these braking techniques to be successful, it is important that your brakes be in good condition. If they are not now, see that they are before setting out on your bike again. Also, make sure the front brake lever is on the same side on all bicycles you ride since your hands will be trained to respond differently from one another.

All of these warnings of hazards may seem overwhelming at first, and they can be, especially since you have to simultaneously read the road and cope with other traffic, but if you practice emergency turning and braking maneuvers and ride alert, it won't be long before recognizing obstacles and taking proper action become automatic. Meanwhile, relax! Riding rigid is more a hindrance than a help. Good bike handling combines alertness of mind with relaxation of body.

Save the Wheels

How many times have you seen a kid ride his balloon tire bike head on into a curb? Perhaps you did it yourself a few times when you were younger. Kids seem to enjoy moving back and forth between sidewalk and street without dismounting or using a driveway. Now that you have outgrown your childhood riding style, you probably don't deal much with curbs, but you still have to cope with potholes, railroad tracks, and other hazards. They can do as much damage to your bike as any curb, especially when encountered at road riding speeds.

There are techniques that can be used to spare your wheels much abuse when encountering unfriendly objects. The first one is very simple. No real skill is required, yet it could make all the difference in having round rims after crossing a set of railroad tracks. It involves shifting the body weight to distribute it more evenly between your bike's wheels than is ordinarily the case.

Roughly speaking, the way most people sit on their bikes, they have close to 50 percent more weight on the rear wheel than the front. This disproportionate weight distribution is great for rear tire traction but deadly for the rim when you hit a bad pothole or bump. The front wheel will usually bounce over the obstacle with its lesser weight, but when the rear wheel hits, the additional body weight bearing down can depress the tire completely to the rim. The rim has no choice but to give way. The result is a flat spot on the rim, which you feel as a rhythmic grabbing of the brakes whenever you apply them. To distribute the weight more evenly as you go over some rough railroad tracks or a couple of unavoidable potholes, get up off the saddle and crouch with knees and elbows flexed, centering your body weight evenly between the two wheels.

Pull Up

Pulling up on the handlebars and pedals is a way to "lighten" the weight on the wheels. Practice this at very slow speeds until you get the hang of it. A low curb or speed-trap bump will help you in your timing and coordination. At a walking pace, ride up to the curb. At the instant before the front tire hits it, jerk up sharply on the handlebars. Essentially you should be lifting the wheel up onto the curb. Do the same thing for the rear wheel. With your crankarms horizontal, jerk up on the pedals the instant before the rear tire touches the curb. This exercise requires a bit of practice, toe straps on the pedals, and a helmet on your head. Timing and coordination are essential, otherwise the opposite of the desired effect may result.

The pull up maneuver is handy for many situations with potholes, bumps, and rough road. With more practice and skill, an experienced cyclist can combine these "pull ups" into a single jump. Cyclo-cross riders do it all the time. American champion Laurence Malone was noted a few years back by the European cycling press for his amazing jump, clearing objects 20 inches high.

Photograph 2–2. Practice jumping your bike over small sticks or other harmless objects before moving up to bigger challenges.

Timing is crucial when jumping your bike. The jerk up on the bars and pedals must be done evenly and at the same instant. To clear objects you must also have sufficient forward momentum. One of our editors absolutely destroyed a rear wheel once trying to jump a curb. He had plenty of height; he simply was not going fast enough. His rear wheel landed squarely on the corner of the curb. Ouch! Take his advice and practice jumping small sticks or expansion cracks before trying to jump something more monumental.

For a racer, jumping like this is very useful since light racing wheels do not always hold up crossing railroad tracks. Perhaps you have seen photographs of European pros jumping over fallen riders and bikes during a pack sprint. We hope you will not have to be quite so acrobatic, but it is a nice feeling to sail over a bad pothole or pile of glass.

If you are an ambitious, daredevil BMX kind of rider, a highly advanced technique for which you may have occasional use is a sideways jump. It can come in handy if you find yourself being forced into a curb during a race or in traffic. After mastering all the other jumping techniques, you will find that jumping sideways is simply a matter of shifting your weight and springing off the saddle in the desired direction. It's important, though, to land with your wheels lined upright—bicycle wheels aren't made for sideways loads.

All of these skills can be useful and will certainly add to your overall confidence and ability as a bike handler. They are worthy of some time and effort. However, while you are in the process of mastering them, you are well advised to mount a pair of old wheels on your bike. There is no point in destroying an expensive pair of rims when you can avoid it. Also, be sure to wear a helmet, maybe knee and elbow pads as well for the fancier maneuvers.

Riding Fast in the City

When it comes to riding in traffic, cyclists seem to crawl along. They complain of being boxed in by the traffic and move cautiously ahead at eight to ten mph, worried about cars overtaking them on the left and the doors of parked cars opening in front of them on the right.

While it certainly is important to exercise caution in traffic, this doesn't necessarily mean you have to ride slowly. In fact, riding at a brisk pace gives drivers behind you much more time to see you and plan their overtaking. And riding far enough over in your lane to keep clear of car doors leaves you more room to maneuver, while also making you visible to drivers both behind and ahead of you.

The easiest way to keep moving quickly in city traffic is by remembering that you are a driver of a vehicle, with the same rights and responsibilities as other drivers. Thinking about this fact should give you confidence. The rules of the road also give you the right to a safe place in which to maneuver as long as you accept the responsibilities involved in respecting other drivers' rights. In every traffic situation, the rules of the road prescribe which driver can go and which driver must yield; for instance, drivers entering the street from driveways must yield to others. To keep moving, it is clearly important to make this rule work for you.

When you are riding along a street and a driver is entering from a driveway or a side street with a stop sign, make yourself visible, assert your right-of-way, establish eye contact, and watch for the car to stop. If it doesn't, then make an emergency maneuver. These techniques guarantee your right-of-way almost 100 percent of the time, but when a driver insists on breaking the law, these techniques also prevent accidents.

Understand that you have the right to use as much of the road width as you need for your safety. Keep clear of the doors of parked cars and places where pedestrians can walk out without your seeing them. You can ride at high speeds safely only when you give yourself enough room. At city traffic speeds, rear-end collisions are extremely rare. If the right lane is too narrow to share side-by-side safely with cars, don't tempt the driver to skim by your elbow. Ride far enough out in the lane so that

Photograph 2–3. Ride far enough out in the lane that you will not be in danger of being struck by an opening car door.

drivers must overtake you by using the next lane. As long as you ride in a straight line down the road, drivers behind you must yield to you, regardless of your position.

　　But drivers behind you cannot predict when you will move sideways in traffic, so you must yield to those already in the lane that you desire to enter. For example, if a stopped bus ahead of you makes it necessary to move left to the next lane so you can keep moving, then traffic already in the lane to your left has the right-of-way. Still, you can almost always keep moving. Don't wait until you've almost reached a stopped vehicle before taking action.

When you are still a couple of hundred feet behind the bus or other stopped vehicle, look back. If there is no traffic in the next lane for a considerable distance behind you, simply move left into the next lane. If there is a car approaching from behind in the next lane, you must get the cooperation of the driver to

Photograph 2–4. Always look behind you to see if traffic is approaching before moving into the next lane.

let you into line. Sometimes simply turning your head is enough to signal to the driver that you wish to move left. Make repeated, quick glances to the rear, so you can also keep track of the situation ahead of you. A left-turn signal is also often helpful.

When you show what you want, most people will be happy to cooperate. If the first driver behind you doesn't, then you have another chance with the second driver. Begin your lane-changing early enough so that you have two chances, then you will almost never be forced to a stop behind a bus, double-parked car, or other obstacle. Even in a case where you are required to yield, you can almost always keep moving.

Photograph 2–5. Use hand signals to make your intentions clear to drivers behind you before turning or changing lanes.

On a multilane street with slow traffic, you may find yourself moving more than one lane to the left to clear stopped traffic and slow, right-turning traffic. Look back and get the cooperation of the driver behind you twice for each lane you cross: once as you move to the other side of the lane you are in and again as you cross the lane line into the new lane. Keep well clear of the bus or other obstacle, just as you keep clear of car doors at the side of the street. Then the bus driver will see you when looking back and can wait for you to pass before moving out into the street again. You will also see pedestrians coming around the front of the bus in time to avoid them.

Choosing Your Routes

Generally, large streets let you ride faster. On main streets, most cross streets will have stop signs, giving you the right-of-way. Traffic light sequences give more time to the main streets. Although there is usually more traffic on main streets, these streets are also straighter, sight lines are longer, and lanes are wider. If you ride slowly, back streets are generally more pleasant, but if you ride fast, main streets allow you to keep up your pace. They are less taxing of your energy and attention, and they are safer for fast travel.

If you have a choice, take a route with fewer intersections. A freeway or expressway with a paved shoulder is one of the safest places you can ride, and you can zoom along at top speed. Of course, you should first make sure that cycling on a freeway is legal in your state. In a city street grid, roads that border railroad lines, freeways, rivers, or industrial areas will have fewer intersections and often less traffic.

Timing Traffic Lights

In a network of two-way streets, the timing of traffic lights is more or less random. Some intersections have four-way walk lights; while these are on, traffic from all directions is stopped by red lights. It is legitimate for you to walk or scoot your bike across a walk light but not to pedal across it.

Where streets are one-way in a grid, traffic lights are usually synchronized to 30 mph. Cars will move steadily, and the drivers will never see a red light. If you are in reasonably good shape, you can maintain a 20-mph pace, riding a half mile or more at a stretch, then waiting 45 seconds, going another half mile, and waiting again. Only one out of each group of several lights will be red for you. In times of light traffic, increase your span between red lights by slowing in midblock for a red light, then accelerating just as the cars begin to move at the intersection behind you. The red light ahead will turn green just as you reach it, traveling at full speed.

A similar trick is to slow or wait at the top of a hill for a red light at the bottom. Use the hill to get you going, instead of wasting it by braking at the bottom. Look for the "don't walk" signal facing you. It will go on well before the yellow light, giving you plenty of notice to slow down in midblock or on a hill. While waiting, look at the traffic signal for the cross street, if you can see it. If it's yellow, the red light facing you will soon turn green. The side street signal is your clue to get into the toe clips and begin moving before your light turns green.

If a light turns yellow just as you reach an intersection—too late to stop—then speed up. Once you have entered an intersection legally, you have right-of-way to clear the intersection. On your bicycle, you may not be moving as fast as other traffic, so when you cross a very wide street, the light may turn from green to yellow to red before you have crossed the intersection. In this instance, glance back, then move closer to the center of the street so drivers waiting at both sides ahead of you in the cross street can see you.

On routes you travel repeatedly, you can often improve your speed by studying the pattern of traffic light changes, planning when to put on full speed and when to relax and catch your breath so you get the largest number of green lights.

Your Best Speed in Traffic

When timing traffic lights, vary your speed to make the most efficient use of your energy. Generally, the best speed in traffic is brisk, to give you the most time to negotiate lane changes with drivers approaching from behind, but stay a bit below your top cruising speed so you'll have a reserve of power to accelerate. Time your interactions with other drivers by slowing down and occasionally speeding up. At this brisk pace, you can usually slow down gently by coasting without wasting energy braking, leaving you a reserve of power to use for quick acceleration when you need it.

When you ride according to the rules of the road, you are much safer because you never appear suddenly in front of anyone as a surprise. Your safety is increased because other drivers are aware of you and can predict your actions. This sane, sensible approach to riding feels good and makes for good relations with your road-sharing neighbors.

Taking Your Place on the Road

When summer arrives, a cyclist's thoughts turn to the open road. When the weekends roll around, some will fasten a light load of food on their bikes and set out on all-day tours and occasionally an overnight camping expedition. Others will equip themselves for more serious touring, spending a week or more of vacation time on the road. But whether it be a cross-country tour or merely a day-trip into the countryside, it is important that every cyclist give some thought on how to make the journey safe.

If you are venturing out into unfamiliar or heavily traveled terrain, you will have to be especially careful to anticipate potential hazards. You will need to continually draw on your best bike handling skills as well as your common sense and your knowledge of traffic laws. You must be prepared to share the road with all types of vehicles. This can be done. Just remember one rule: use courtesy when you can and be assertive if you must. Then take the road with confidence.

Coping with Traffic

The rule about where to ride is the same for the open-road environment as it is for in town: keep just to the right of moving traffic if the lane is wide enough to share side-by-side with cars. If the lane isn't wide enough, ride far enough toward the center so motorists will not be tempted to skim by your elbow. Instead, they will have to move partway into the next lane to overtake, or they will have to slow down and follow you if overtaking is impossible.

You'll find the biggest differences between riding in the city and in an open-road environment are that open-road traffic is generally faster, and roads are bordered with shoulders rather than curbs or parked cars. If the shoulder surface is not as smooth as the traffic lane surface, then as a general rule you should avoid riding on the shoulder. However, you can usually ride closer to a shoulder—even a gravel or dirt shoulder—than to a curb or parked car. If you have to swerve suddenly onto the shoulder to avoid a stone in the road or some other obstacle, you can still keep your balance. You can ride as close as one foot to the edge of the pavement and allow motorists to overtake you in a lane little or no wider than the roads in town. You can also give the motorists the somewhat greater clearance required by their higher speed and wind blast.

If for any reason you do pull off onto a dirt or gravel shoulder, brake lightly and avoid turning sharply. On returning to the traffic lane, remember you are required to yield to traffic already in the lane. Also, be especially careful of the edge of the pavement since it is often higher than the shoulder and can catch your front wheel and dump you. Steer sharply across the grade if necessary, or ride along until you find a place where the shoulder is level with the pavement before moving back on it.

Some highways and most freeways have well-paved, clean shoulders. These make for easier riding. Even if traffic is heavy, you can ride on the shoulder without constantly worrying about wandering into gravel. But when riding on a wide shoulder, don't ride all the way over at the right edge. Instead, ride relatively close to the traffic—about four feet to the right of the traffic when it is traveling at highway speed and about three feet to the right when it is traveling at lower speeds. In this position, you will be more visible to drivers pulling out from cross roads. Also, drivers behind you preparing to make right turns will be less likely to try to go around your left side and cut you off.

If a driver does attempt to cut you off, you will see the car just as it begins to turn. You can then turn right with it and avoid an accident. If you were farther to the right, the car would have already turned into your path before you saw it. If the shoulder is very wide and traffic is moving slowly in the lane

Photograph 2–6. When highway traffic is heavy, you can ride on a clean shoulder, but stay close enough to the traffic that you remain clearly visible to drivers entering or leaving the road.

to the left of you, an impatient driver may sometimes (rarely) decide to pull off onto the shoulder and pass illegally on the right. In this case, too, it is safer to be close to the traffic.

Highway riding is not always very pleasant because traffic may be heavy. Yet it is important for you to distinguish between an unpleasant and a dangerous situation. A highway or freeway with a broad, paved shoulder and few intersections affords a safe place to ride and is often shorter and less hilly than an alternate route. Your choice of a route depends on whether you are in a hurry or wish to have a more pleasant, recreational ride.

Of course, sometimes the highway—or freeway—may be the only available route. Recognizing this, several states have struck down prohibitions against bicycles on their rural freeways. If bicyclists in your state point out the need, your state might be next! (Note: cycling on freeways is still illegal in some states so be sure to check with local police before setting out on your trip.)

The Straight and Narrow

Many of your travels, however, will probably be on narrow, secondary highways and rural roads. These routes usually have more curves, steeper hills, more intersections, and poorer pavement than the bigger roads. When traffic on one of these secondary roads is heavy, it is the worst kind of road—unpleasant, annoying, and downright dangerous for cyclists and motorists alike. Traffic on roads of this type can back up for miles behind a slow-moving bicycle. In this instance, courtesy and the law dictate you pull over and let motorists pass. Yet many of the smaller roads have less traffic, and these are the pleasant roads that bicyclists seek out for scenery and quiet.

Still, even a lightly traveled smaller road has its own particular hazards, which often require special attention. The hills, curves, and bumps place greater demands on your bike handling. Don't underrate these hazards. Half of all serious bicycle accidents are single-bike accidents; bike-bike, bike-dog, and bike-car accidents account for most of the other half. Bike-car accidents are about 18 percent of the total, but head-on and rear-end collisions, rare most everywhere else, are most common on the two-lane country roads. A narrower road requires more care from you and motorists to deal with one another safely.

Navigating Safely

On a narrow, two-lane rural road with a clear shoulder where you can be sure there is no traffic approaching from the front, it is okay for you to stay fairly close to the right edge. This way, motorists coming from behind won't have to deviate much to the left. But when there is traffic approaching from the front, it is important to take control of the situation. You must make a clear decision whether you consider it safe for drivers behind you to overtake.

When the traffic from the front is still distant—in other words, well before overtaking becomes questionable for a driver close behind you—look back and see whether there is traffic behind you. If a vehicle is farther back, so that it will reach you at the same time as traffic from ahead, you should clearly signal to the driver behind you to slow and follow you. Move farther toward the middle of the lane. When a driver is a long distance behind you, your best signal is your position in the lane. Your whole body serves as a signal.

Yes, you are forcing the driver behind you to slow and follow, but this is only what the law requires the driver to do when overtaking is unsafe. Drivers know this, and most are perfectly willing to cooperate. What you should not do is to pull over as far to the right as you can and invite the driver to overtake you when it is unsafe.

As the driver behind you gets closer, you can put communication on a more personal basis. Make a slow signal or give an acknowledging turn of the head, and when it becomes safe for the driver to overtake, wave him by as you pull back to the right. This is one situation in which a helmet-mounted rearview mirror can be especially useful. It allows you to check on the reaction of the driver behind you without diverting attention from the traffic in front.

Any traffic from the front requires frequent attention on a two-lane rural road. A lone driver is likely to be less careful

Photograph 2–7. On narrow two-lane roads, it is important that you use your position on the road to discourage traffic from passing in dangerous situations.

about keeping to the right than in town. When traffic is light, the temptation to cut corners is strong. And be especially attentive when a string of cars is approaching from the front. A driver may pull out into your lane to pass, not looking for anything as small as a bicyclist. When this happens, you may have no choice but to leave the road.

Drivers approaching from the front over hilltops and around blind curves are generally more careful about crossing the centerline, but in these situations, it is not safe for a driver behind you to merge even a little bit across the centerline to overtake you. Some will try it anyway if given the opportunity. Therefore, you should assume that a car is approaching from the front, even when you cannot see one. If one does suddenly appear, the driver from behind will probably pull back to the right and risk running into you rather than chance a head-on collision.

Before you come to a blind curve, glance back to make sure there's room, then pull farther into the lane as a clear signal that a driver behind you must slow down. And when approaching a blind intersection or driveway, also pull farther into the

Photograph 2–8. When approaching a blind curve to the right, pull toward the left side of the lane to encourage traffic behind you to slow down and to make it easier for you to see and be seen by traffic heading your way.

lane in case a driver pulls out to take a look. On a blind right curve with a wall or vegetation on the right, you may have to pull most of the way to the left side of the lane so a driver approaching from behind can see you as soon as possible.

This position also makes it possible for you to see farther ahead than the driver behind you. The driver will appreciate your courtesy in serving as a lookout. As soon as you see that the way is clear, pull back to the right and let the driver by. You can give a wave-by, too, but in this case, since the driver cannot see ahead, be very sure there's plenty of room for him to overtake you before waving him by.

Climbing a Hill

When you are climbing, approaching a hilltop, the driver behind you also cannot see ahead, but at your slow climbing speed, you do not need as much room to maneuver as you normally would. You can keep farther to the right to let motorists overtake you from behind. Give the motorist this advantage if you decide the lane is wide enough for overtaking.

When you are just beyond the crest of the hill, motorists behind you cannot see you as soon as they normally would. There are several ways to deal with this problem. You can alert motorists to your presence before you crest the hill. In this situation, bright clothing is most helpful so a distant driver takes notice of you. If the driver behind you is fairly distant, you might temporarily pull farther into your lane to make yourself more visible.

However, once you have crested the hill and dropped out of sight, keep to the right for a few seconds until you have built up speed and the sight distance has opened up behind you. It is also helpful to hold your head high and to wear a brightly colored helmet. The preferred tactic to make the fastest overall speed is to stand up and spring past the top of a hill. Use a low enough gear going up so you have the strength remaining for a sprint, and your head's bobbing from side to side will make it easier to be seen. If you do a lot of riding on narrow roads in rolling country, it may make sense for you to use a safety flag as well.

Once you get going down the hill, you will often travel as fast as cars do or nearly as fast. When you encounter curves, you lean and continue at the same speed, but cars don't. Motorists hold their speed down so baggage and unseatbelted passengers don't slide from one side of the car to the other, so keep a good distance from the car ahead in case the driver brakes sharply. And when your downhill speed approaches that of the cars, ride in the *middle* of the right lane. You need the extra maneuvering room to avoid pavement irregularities. You'll want to make the corners a bit less sharp, too, by cutting across from one side of your lane to the other. So don't sneak up next to a car in the same lane, and don't let one sneak up next to you. At your downhill speed, you're not delaying the motorist behind you much anyway, if at all.

In summary, the correct lane position for you on a rural road may be anywhere from the right edge to (occasionally) left of the center of the right lane. The correct lane position depends on the lane width and the distance at which you can see and be seen. Be conscious of which position is appropriate.

Look ahead to see whether you might have to move closer to the center of the lane and then look back while you still have plenty of time. Make your move when the car behind you is far enough back for the driver to react smoothly to your new position. These manuevers may sound difficult at first, but like anything else, it's just a matter of time until you master them. They can make the difference between an enjoyable summertime tour and a disaster.

Part Three
Developing Good Racing Form

Any Cyclist Can Benefit from Riding Racer-Smooth

A seasoned racer is easy to spot because of his smooth pedaling style. Such fluid form is something the competitive cyclist works methodically to develop. It enables him (or her) to stay fresher during a hard race than someone with a choppy style of pedaling because smooth pedaling is more energy efficient. Whether you are commuting to work, riding a century, or competing in a national championship, smooth pedaling will enable you to arrive at your destination fresher, with more energy than would otherwise be possible.

Efficiency at any speed could be the topic of a long discussion, but our focus in this chapter is on efficient riding at moderate speeds. What works to make the bike go fastest in an all-out sprint is not necessarily most efficient in general. There is going to be some wasted motion at top speed: the rider is out of the saddle, and bike and body are thrashing from side to side. When the finish line is just ahead, that is what gets you there the quickest. But at moderate speeds—80 percent of maximum effort or below, let's say—you can ride most efficiently by putting the bulk of your energy into spinning the pedals smoothly.

A fluid pedaling motion is valuable for all types of cyclists. It is absolutely essential for the aspiring racer. Without it, he will be at a loss when the pace picks up and the real "crunch" develops. For the tourist or even casual rider, an effortless spin will make all rides seem shorter and much more enjoyable. With proper pedal action, a great deal of saddle soreness and upper body fatigue can be avoided.

The Test

When we talk about smooth pedaling, we are referring to a relaxed, fluid, circular pedaling cadence of 80 to 110 rpm (count complete revolutions of one foot). This cadence has proved to be the most energy efficient. When you develop a smooth 110-rpm pedaling motion, your own observations will confirm its value.

To test your present ability at pedaling smoothly, start down from the top of a hill or sloping grade, using a small gear. As smoothly as possible, work the rpm up from 60 to 80 to 100 to 110, and so on. If you can keep 110 rpm, spinning without bouncing around on the saddle, you are doing very well. A cadence this high exaggerates your pedal action and also any problems you might have with it.

Top racing cyclists can spin smoothly up to 150 rpm and higher. U.S.C.F. National Coaching Director Eddie Borysewicz has sprinters doing workouts on stationary bikes at zero resistance, pedaling as high as 300 rpm. Even though they can't do this very smoothly, it helps the riders develop their fast-twitch muscle fibers—what we call "snap."

Common Causes of Inefficient Pedaling

Bouncing

This is probably the most common problem. If you find yourself bouncing off the saddle at your maximum rpm, it is probably only an amplification of your bodily movements at 60 to 80 rpm. This bouncing occurs when pedaling is not in a circular motion; on the downward motion of the pedal, you reach the bottom and continue to push down. The effect of this is a momentary lifting off the saddle. Bouncing is a prime energy waster. Racers often refer to this as "pedaling squares."

Photograph 3–1. Working out on a stationary bike, with little or no resistance, will help to develop the ability to pedal circles with good spin.

Rocking

A rocking or even wiggling motion of the hips or upper body is probably from improper seat height or position. This can easily be checked with the help of a friend or coach. With the bike stationary and your friend standing behind you, sit comfortably in a riding position. Backpedal very slowly, making certain that at the bottom of each pedal stroke there is a slight bend in the knee and your toes are not pointed. Your friend should check to see that your hips stay stationary and do not rock from side to side with each pedal stroke. In most cases, the rocking motion will be eliminated by lowering your saddle.

Swaying

Do you find it difficult to ride a straight line? If so, the problem may be improper movement in the upper part of your body, movement caused by excessive bodily rigidity. Swaying of the upper body is often transferred to the handlebars and creates an erratic path and unsteady steering. The tenseness behind the swaying also is a great drain on your energy.

Tense shoulders and stiff arms can tire you in two ways. First, tensing the muscles requires energy. Any muscles you don't need to use should be kept loose and relaxed, saving and conserving energy for when you might need it—for hills, sprints, or a hard day at work. Second, stiff arms and shoulders transfer all the road vibration and shock to the body, fatiguing it unnecessarily.

Your entire upper body should be kept limber and relaxed, though still alert. Riding in this way, you will find both that your wrists and arms absorb a lot of road vibration and that it is easier to ride a straight line. After all, there is no sense in covering more ground than you have to by weaving back and forth across the road. Even a small amount of weaving adds up over time. The only way to really deal with this problem is to make a mental effort to relax and loosen your arms, shoulders, and neck. Very quickly this will become natural without the need of mental reminders.

Riding relaxed is not only more energy efficient than riding tense, it is also safer. Quite often, racing in the tight quarters of a pack, riders bump shoulders, elbows, and handlebars. Riding stiff-armed in that type of environment invariably leads to accidents.

The Technique

After evaluating your pedaling style to determine your problem or problems and checking your seat height to make sure it is correct, concentrate on the basics of smooth spinning.

Think circles and attempt to pedal that way. Try to visualize the entire motion as you feel the muscles gently working throughout a 360-degree cycle. When you're training, find a gear that is comfortable, then gear down one (say from a 42 × 15 to a 42 × 17). This will exaggerate your pedaling just enough so that you will be aware and concentrate on it.

If your problem is rocking or swaying of the upper body, and you've already checked your seat height, try to be aware of your upper body. An easy way to monitor your movements is to watch your shadow on the pavement. With enough sunshine and attention, you will soon be riding smoother and more relaxed.

Many racers start their early season training on a fixed gear (60 to 67 inches) because it leaves no choice but to pedal smoothly. Riding rollers will also help immensely in smoothing out any rough spots. Here again, try to use a gear just slightly lower than what is comfortable.

Photograph 3–2. Rebecca Twigg (left) is described by coach Michael Kolin as one of the smoothest pedalers he has ever seen. Technical excellence has helped boost Rebecca to the top level of women's cycling.

Basic pedaling, like any other aspect of cycling technique, cannot be neglected even after mastering it. If you neglect to use it, you will lose it. But once you develop a fluid, efficient pedal motion, it takes only occasional attention to keep it perfect. Racers often refer to a feeling of "floating" over spinning pedals. Once you become comfortable with spinning your pedals rapidly, maintaining an efficient 80- to 110-rpm cadence will feel easy. Riding your bike will become more enjoyable when you discover the added energy you gain from pedaling smoothly.

Improve Your Technique with Fixed-Gear Training

There is no more effective way to begin a cycling season than to spend some time riding a "fixed" wheel. European racers routinely ride 500 to 1,000 miles in a fixed gear as preliminary training. For the serious racing or touring cyclist, the benefits of such training cannot be overemphasized. If the training is undertaken at the beginning of the season, results will be immediately apparent.

A fixed-gear bicycle is one that has no freewheeling mechanism. A single cog is threaded onto the rear hub, and this fixed cog drives the wheel. The most significant difference between a fixed-gear bicycle and one with a freewheel is that the cranks of the former always turn in a direct relationship to the motion of the rear wheel. So if the bicycle is moving, the cranks are turning. You cannot stop pedaling to let the bike freewheel. Though this might seem a bother, it is in fact the very principle behind fixed-gear training.

Training with a fixed gear offers several benefits. It helps you achieve the following objectives:

- establish optimum position on the bicycle
- acquire round pedaling technique
- develop suppleness and spin ("snap")
- improve balance and agility on the bicycle

By pursuing these goals, you develop good technique, and good technique not only looks good and feels good, it is also the most efficient way to power your bicycle.

Position

Since a fixed gear forces you to pedal constantly, incompatibilities between you and your bike, which might otherwise go unnoticed, become more apparent. Here's why. The natural and unconscious response of the body as it begins to feel discomfort is to relax and stop pedaling. However, this discomfort is often attributable to incorrect position rather than excessive exertion. Without the continuous pedaling enforced by the fixed gear, you might never be aware of poor bike setup, even though it has been detracting from your efficiency and possibly causing you injury.

For example, if your saddle is too high you can still go indefinitely on a freewheel without realizing it. There are enough opportunities to stand and coast, even just for a period of two or three pedal strokes, on any ride. So your body has a chance to relax the affected aching area. With a fixed gear, however, this is much less likely to happen. You don't get the little "breaks" you get on a freewheel. If your seat is too high, your body soon feels it. The same is true for the position of shoe cleats, handlebar height, stem length, and all the other mechanical adjustments. While you can get a pretty good idea of correct position on a freewheel bike, a fixed gear helps you establish optimum position more precisely.

Round Pedaling

To a certain extent, a role reversal occurs in fixed-gear training because the pedals are in constant motion. The cyclist is obliged to follow the motion of the cranks instead of always controlling it. Since this motion is round, smooth, and constant, good pedaling technique evolves. At first the motion seems awkward, but with practice the body adapts. Rather than a pumping action, which delivers power only on the downstroke (some people call this "pedaling square"), you develop pedal action, which puts pressure on the crankarms uniformly throughout their entire revolution. Round pedaling is not only more efficient, it is also necessary if you want to increase your ability to spin.

Spinning

With a fixed gear, pedal cadence will vary according to the terrain. On climbs, the gear feels big; on descents, it feels uncomfortably small. This variance, particularly the short, high rpm bursts required on short descents, develops suppleness and spin. Concentrate on smooth, round pedaling with the upper body relaxed. You'll develop "snap," necessary for jumping away from the field in a race, bridging gaps, and winning sprints. Even if you're loaded down with bags out on a tour rather than in a race, spinning the pedals is still the most efficient way for you to ride.

Balance and Agility

The simplicity of the fixed gear puts you in much closer connection with your bicycle than is ordinarily the case. Acceleration and deceleration can be read by your legs. You can feel the power of your own momentum as you work against the motion of the cranks while decelerating. Because the pedals always turn while the bike is in motion, you'll have to pedal over railroad tracks, through turns, and in all other situations where you would otherwise not pedal. In such situations, you'll learn the limitations of your bicycle and your abilities, and you'll maximize your agility on the bike.

How to Train

The fixed-gear training period should be two weeks to a month in duration, immediately prior to the regular cycling season. Your emphasis during this period is on developing good form and preparing your body for specialized training. If you live in a cold climate and have spent a couple of months off the bike, be careful. Over-enthusiasm when resuming strenuous activity after a lay-off can sometimes be worse than doing nothing at all. Lack of fitness together with bad weather can easily create a situation where an over-zealous cyclist is sick in bed, rather than coming into form.

Approach your first ride on a fixed-gear bike with a healthy mix of caution and attention. Don't tighten the toe straps until you feel comfortable doing so. Practice decelerating from speed to get used to backpedaling against the action of the cranks. Make several low-speed figure-eight turns. Get used to pedaling over railroad tracks, potholes, and anything else you usually coast over without thinking. You'll inevitably be confronted with these situations, and the reflective actions brought about by thousands of miles on a freewheel will not apply. Remember, as long as the bike is moving, the cranks are moving.

To make certain that the sprocket is tightly threaded onto your rear wheel, find the steepest short hill in your neighborhood and climb it as fast as you can. The object here is to get the sprocket on tightly, so stomp really hard on the pedals.

After you've gotten used to the feel of the fixed gear, take whatever wrenches you'll need and go for a short ride on a flat to rolling circuit. Make positional changes as necessary. In most instances, if you've reached the point in your training that you're considering fixed gears, your position should already be pretty well established. Adjustments now are the final modifications to a machine that is uniquely suited to your body. Make all adjustments in very small increments, say less than a half centimeter at a time. Dramatic modifications usually prove counterproductive. Take along the tool kit until you feel you've arrived at the optimum position.

Individual training programs vary, although long distances aren't usually advisable. Between 15 and 30 miles is a good distance. Going out every day, even if it's only a short ride, is much better than piling on mileage only on the weekends. On these daily rides, pay close attention to position and technique. Concentrate on pedaling round. If the crankarms are pushing your legs through the upstroke, you're not pedaling round. Forget about the downstroke. Concentrate on pulling the pedal across the bottom of the stroke, using the hamstring muscles to pull on the upstroke, pushing the pedal over the top of the pedal stroke. Always bear in mind that the object is a fluid, continuous motion.

Rounding your pedaling increases your ability to spin. To develop this, select a downhill stretch for daily practice. As you begin the descent, you'll experience pleasant, effortless pedaling as gravity begins to assume your workload. However, the cranks will turn increasingly faster, eventually reaching a point at which you will find the rhythm of the pedals difficult and finally impossible to maintain. If your pedal motion is choppy and uneven, the point at which you can no longer keep up with the pedals will arrive much sooner than if it's fluid and smooth. A conscious effort to use the hamstring muscles in the upstroke is especially helpful in developing spin. Hamstrings, at the back side of your thigh, are used to a much greater extent at high rpms. You'll find that by keeping the upper body relaxed and by concentrating on a smooth, continuous pedal motion, your ability to spin will increase measureably.

Muscles work in opposition. Besides developing spin, downhill sessions can be used to develop opposing muscle groups. Initially, when you reach the point at which you can't pedal as fast as the cranks are turning, you'll bounce all over the bike and have to use the brakes to bring the bike under control. As you become progressively more sure of yourself, work against the action of the cranks to slow yourself down. Use the brakes only in emergency situations. By doing this, you'll develop muscles that are ordinarily little used. At the conclusion of the training period, you may find it helpful and fun to keep a second bicycle as a fixed-gear bike. This is particularly useful to loosen up tight legs on days following long rides or hard races.

When you climb on your fixed-gear bike, never forget that you are not equipped with a freewheel and that the cranks will always move in a direct relationship to the motion of the rear wheel. If the wheel is moving, the cranks are moving, regardless

Photograph 3–3. Track racers must develop a smooth, even pedaling motion in order to develop high speeds without crashing.

of what you want to do. Just as the bicycle is a very efficient machine that converts your energy into motion, it is equally efficient in converting momentum into thrust on the cranks. And, if you choose to lock your leg in the six o'clock position, as in going around a turn, the efficient machine will catapult you into space. Anticipate pedaling through turns; slow down or go wide enough so you don't plant the inside pedal. Stay relaxed and pedal smoothly in all situations.

Fixed-Gear Conversion

It's an easy 20-minute job to change your road bike into a fixed-gear vehicle. You'll only need one or two items of new equipment, costing ten dollars or less each: a track cog and perhaps a track chain. You've probably noticed that track bikes have their own special hubs for fixed-gear riding, but you won't need one of those hubs, only a cog. The track cog is threaded, and it screws onto the threads meant for a freewheel. Just be sure to get a track cog with the same threading as your hub; for example, English hub, English track cog.

You will have to decide what size cog to get. Since they're made mostly for strong competitors, most cogs in your local bike shop are likely to be too small for training. For example, the largest cog Shimano lists in their catalog has only 16 teeth. SunTour offers a 17-tooth cog, and Zeus makes them up to 19 teeth. What you want to wind up with is (for most reasonably fit cyclists) a gear in the low 60-inch range. Cyclists with less brute strength for hill climbing will need a lower fixed-gear, but frankly, they'll find it tedious on flats and downhills. You'll want to avoid the expense of buying a new chainwheel if you can, of course, so select a cog that works well with one of the chainwheels you already have. For example, a 40-tooth chainwheel and a 17-tooth track cog give you a 63½-inch gear.

You'll probably have to buy a new chain (though if you can find narrow cogs, you'll avoid this expense). Track cogs are customarily wider then derailleur cogs, and they require a chain of ⅛-inch width instead of ³⁄₃₂-inch width. (There is one exception to this: Maeda SunTour makes track cogs for derailleur chains.) You can buy a track chain for this purpose or borrow a chain from the nearest 3-speed bike. Either will do.

After buying the equipment, you're ready to begin the conversion. Here are the steps to follow.

1. Remove the cluster from the rear wheel and spin on the fixed cog, making sure that the hub and the cog are compatibly threaded.
2. Remove front and rear derailleurs, cables, and shift levers. (This is optional, but if you choose to leave this equipment on, tighten down the adjusting screws so that the derailleurs are out of the way and immobilized.)
3. If the chain you have is usable, remove it and shorten it so that it fits loosely around the chainring and cog but not so loosely that it's possible for the chain to jump a tooth. (Small increments of slop can be taken up by moving the rear wheel

backward in the dropouts.) Or replace your chain with a track chain.

4. Check to see that the wheel is straight in the dropouts and that the quick-release skewer is tight.

Once you have completed these four steps, you are ready to get started on your fixed-gear training.

Learn to Read a Race and Let Conditions Determine Tactics

A chilly, damp St. Patrick's Day wind blew steadily across the course as a field of top racers lined up for a 90-mile stage of the Spring, 1984, Frito-Lay Tour of Texas. Appropriately, the stage's starting point was the little town of Dublin, Texas. The low grey clouds that hung over the racers' heads also contributed to the old-world atmosphere—this could easily have been a race through the Irish countryside.

But the clouds didn't worry the racers as much as that nasty crosswind. The experienced riders in the pack knew it would dictate the outcome of the race. As the pack paraded out of town at a controlled 15-mph pace, the "big guns" were poised like predatory cats on the bumper of the pace car, ready to spring. When the pace car sped up, marking the end of the controlled period, there was an instant explosion of attacks from the lead riders. Everyone else went dashing for the right-hand side of the road to try to find a draft from the crosswind.

The lead riders formed a diagonal echelon extending from the center line of the road to the right-hand gutter. Only 15 riders who could fit in this angled paceline were able to receive any protection from the wind. Traditional "drafting," where one rider tucks in directly behind another, was useless. This was evidenced by the 100 riders strung out behind the echelon, all fighting the wind on their own. It was only a matter of time before these riders would begin to crack from all that lonesome work chasing the leaders.

Indeed, the attacks were so aggressive and the crosswind so strong, that in just two miles the race was over for everyone except the riders who had fought their way into that lead echelon. A split developed, and the main field was soon dropped. Those in that lead group had "read the race" correctly, and it paid off. Reading a race is an intellectual process that can save your legs a lot of glycogen. It is the ability to correctly formulate and apply your tactics according to the prevailing conditions of the race.

On this day, reading the weather was the key to a successful ride. On another day, it could be topography and race course layout that dictate the final standings. A long, steep climb in a race will often spawn a winning breakaway, and by simply knowing where and how long the climbs in a race are, you'll stand a better chance of staying with the leaders. Narrow or bumpy roads can also crack a race open and are worthy of some prerace consideration.

There is a famous climb in Belgium that the world's best pro riders think about constantly during their prerace preparations and then do their best to forget during the rest of the year. It's the treacherous "Koppenburg," a short, steep, narrow, cobbled climb that never fails to blow the field apart. Every year, a rider somewhere in the field crashes on the slippery cobblestones, effectively clogging the eight-foot-wide road for everyone behind. Consequently, there is a mad dash every year to see who can get to this climb first so as not to be caught behind the inevitable crash. The riders who get there before the pileup always constitute the race's winning "breakaway," while everyone behind either ends up chasing in vain or heading for the showers.

The history of that Belgian race enables the racers to know just what to expect each year. So, too, can you learn from the history of the race you are about to compete in—if it has one. Find out before the race begins how the event went last year. Did the field break up during the race? If so, find out when, why,

Photograph 3–4. A breakaway often starts during a long, steep climb.

and who orchestrated the break. Is he back again this year? Who else is here? Learn as much as you can about your competition, their strengths, weaknesses, and racing histories.

Brain over Brawn

By reading a race properly, a weaker cyclist can win over a stronger one. A thinking athlete, the one who is always con-

Photograph 3–5. The experienced racer always tries to stay in touch with the race leaders and is prepared to join a breakaway when a serious one develops.

scious of what is happening in the race, will always have an advantage over the "horsepower" riders, who simply go as fast as they can, for as long as they can.

A thinking rider knows how to interpret the things that happen during a race. Quite often in a criterium, for example, a break will take off but only stay away for half a lap. The next one might last a bit longer, and then one group might stay away for a few laps before being reeled in by the pack. If this trend continues, you can bet that soon, one will take off and stay away.

Your job is to watch these breakaways while sheltered from the wind in the peleton until the real one occurs, and then jump on. If you observe that lap after lap no one is able to establish a significant gap on the field, you should save your strength for what will most likely be a field sprint at the end. By expending some mental energy and trying to read the race, it is possible for you to save yourself a lot of leg power and still end up as the winner.

Part Four
Advanced Techniques

Descending—Fast and Safely

If climbing a mountain is hard work, descending the other side is the big payoff. The only thing more enjoyable than gliding effortlessly down a mountainside on your bike is maybe going a bit faster; it can be a sort of personal roller coaster thrill ride.

At first glance, there does not seem to be a whole lot to descending—sitting on the bike and coasting downhill with the only apparent obstacle being corners for which you might have to brake. Descending safely and descending fast don't necessarily have to be two different things. But there is much more than meets the eye to descending both quickly and safely. The temptation to laugh at danger must be discarded in favor of careful, practiced judgment and a sober awareness of the risk!

For these very reasons, fast descents can be an important racing tactic. There is a "descending story" about the legendary Eddy Merckx (whether it is true or not, we can't say). It seems that on one particular stage of a past Tour de France, Merckx crested the top of a mountain with one rider staying with him. As the two racers approached a series of dangerously steep downhill switchbacks, Merckx's companion reached down and loosened his toe straps. He was thinking that if they should crash, he would be able to get out of his pedals quickly. Merckx saw this and "attacked" (sped up) out of a corner, and the other rider never caught him.

Training for Descents

Being able to descend hills safely and quickly is not something a cyclist can take for granted. Like everything else, you have to work at it to get good. Since the straightaways involve mostly the use of aerodynamic tuck for reaching maximum velocity, the corners are what require the most attention. If you're not familiar with the road, you will have to trust your instantaneous judgment, your bike handling ability, and the highway engineer who built the road!

Corners on hills, for the most part, should be ridden like any other (see the discussion in the separate chapter on cornering). Before you ever reach the corner, you have to start "setting up" for it. First establish your position on the road or "line" for the corner. The line will guide you through the corner with a minimum amount of braking. For a hard corner, this usually means going from the far side of the road opposite the corner, then diving into the corner close to the apex and then riding out to the far side of the road again. (But don't ride into oncoming traffic on an open road!)

With many descents, however, the corners come in rapid succession. Alexi Grewal, the 1984 Olympic champion from Aspen, Colorado, is very familiar with this. "You need to think about the second corner ahead of you. As you come out of one corner, you have to leave room to set up for the next corner." You don't want to be caught without enough room to negotiate a corner.

Setting up for a corner also means having your speed under control before you enter it; braking hard on a tight corner can impair bike handling and control. On the hardest part of a corner where you and the bike are leaning most, it's safer not to use the brakes. Additionally, if to stay on the pavement you have to continue to brake hard while exiting a corner, either your line was wrong or you were going too fast.

The danger of losing control on a corner increases greatly when the road is rough. Quite often mountain roads resemble washboards on the corners. If you should try to brake hard on a bumpy corner like that, your wheels will bounce across the road surface and not respond to your commands. Take the cor-

Photograph 4–1. Cornering on descents involves setting up a line and leaning into the turn, using a minimum amount of braking.

ners slower with rough road surfaces until you can accurately judge the characteristics of your bike under those conditions.

Lean, Then Lean More

A winding descent is the best place to illustrate the technique of leaning into a corner for steering. The bike goes in the direction it is being leaned. The more the lean, the harder (sharper) the turn. The lean is the primary means of steering, while the handlebars are the fine tuning. So the ultimate in fast cornering is to use the maximum safe angle of lean at a speed that allows you "just enough room" as you exit the corner.

To obtain the most stable position while moving through tight corners, lean your body a bit more than your bike. This will keep your bike more upright with tire traction more secure, while it lowers your center of gravity. One look at a motorcycle racer cornering, with his knee almost touching the ground, confirms the validity of this technique.

Alexi Grewal concurs: "When you're flying down a mountain, you've got to lean hard into the corners. If the corner gets real tight, lean even harder. If you find yourself running out of road . . . well . . . just keep leaning." Laying the bike down is a more sensible alternative than flying off the road and perhaps off a cliff.

When you face a difficult situation, one of your greatest enemies is your own fear. Many times riders who are negotiating a tight corner panic halfway through and crash unnecessarily. As former Olympic development team member Mark Frise says, "It's all guts until you get into trouble, then it's all skill." Skill is something you acquire with time and experience.

Perhaps the most fearless and skilled descenders on the professional racing circuit are the Czechoslovakians. They are famous throughout Europe for gaining incredible amounts of time on steep and dangerous downhills, but even they make mistakes sometimes. Racer Thomas Prehn recalls cresting the top of a hard English climb about a half minute behind the leaders and about 30 seconds in front of three Czechs. About a mile or so down the fast descent he was passed by three speeding, wild and crazy Czechs. His own speed was terrifying enough on the narrow twisting roads, so he didn't try to stay with them. A few more hard corners passed before Prehn came across the three of them picking themselves up off the pavement and out of the bushes.

The moral of the story, says Prehn with a chuckle, is that crashing slows you down considerably. It's better to be safe than sorry.

Aero-Tuck

To go faster on a straightaway, after you have spun your top gear out, get into a tuck to decrease your wind resistance.

The aerodynamic position will make a noticeable difference in your speed. We recommend, however, that you stick with the standard tuck and not try anything fancy. With your crankarms horizontal, pull your knees together and crouch down with your chin close to the stem and your hands on the tops of the bars right next to the stem. Keep your elbows together. If you need more control for cornering or braking, stay in the tucked position but put your hands on the drops and fingertips on the brake levers.

With steep or long twisting descents be aware that constant use of the brakes will overheat the rims. (If you need to keep the brakes on, you should come out of your tuck and take advantage of air drag to help slow you down.) Overheating the rims can soften tubular tire glue and cause the air in the tire to expand enough to make it blow out. These things happen rarely, but be aware of them, especially if you're touring with a loaded bike, in which case you will use the brakes even more. Try to pump the brakes lightly rather than keeping the pressure on over a long period of time.

Tourists know that descending with loaded panniers takes a little getting used to. On corners, the weight gives you more straight-line inertia, pulling the bike to the outside of the corner. Packing your weight low gives you more stability, and mid-frame packs seem to affect handling the least. We wouldn't suggest doing any aerodynamic tucks when using handlebar bags. They make steering a bit shaky, and besides, they have an effect similar to a windbreak.

Advanced Racing Technique

If you're really into fast, radical descending, try doing "slingshots" off a friend or teammate. This technique is especially useful if you get away with one or two other riders in a race. The rider in front tucks and descends with the rider behind in his draft. The drafting rider will pick up speed since he has less wind resistance. He will speed up to the front rider's rear wheel

Photograph 4–2. Touring cyclists need to anticipate the effect of handlebar bags and panniers on their bikes' steering and to modify their technique accordingly.

and at the last moment swing out and come flying by. The rider who was in front then jumps into the draft and starts the "slingshot" process over again. Speeds are much faster with this combined effort.

If you are just getting started in cycling and not so sure of your judgment on corners, follow someone you know is good down a curving descent, keeping a safe distance between you and your partner. This way you will learn the proper line for cornering while leaving yourself time to react if you should see that the cyclist in front of you has made a mistake.

Finally, here is the most important bit of advice we have to offer you for making radical descents. Know what you are doing and don't make any mistakes!

Cornering for Racers

A story is told of Eddy Merckx, probably the greatest professional racer ever, about how he cornered. It seems that none of the other pro riders liked to follow Merckx around corners in criteriums because he would ride a little slower and safer than the rest, relying on his overwhelming strength and speed to regain any lost distance. He could, of course, corner as fast or faster than anyone else when he wanted to but generally chose to ride more cautiously. All of us, racers and nonracers alike, can benefit from practicing certain techniques of cornering that Eddy Merckx mastered.

Rule number one and most important: don't pedal through a sharp corner, and always keep your inside pedal in the up position! If you should have your inside pedal down while coasting or pedaling through a corner, you stand a good chance of hitting a pedal on the pavement. Hitting a pedal hard lifts the rear wheel off the ground a bit—a dangerous and costly mistake while negotiating a high-speed corner when tire traction is crucial. Many riders have crashed for just this reason.

Photograph 4–3. Don't pedal through a corner, and keep your inside pedal up so it does not scrape the pavement and send you crashing.

The Line

Taking the proper "line" is really what cornering is all about. This refers to the path you travel through a corner. The ideal line is the one that can be safely negotiated with the minimum amount of lost speed.

Finding this imaginary line through a corner is not that difficult. Let's say you're in a criterium and approaching a corner at a speed that's going to necessitate hitting the brakes. The less you use the brakes, the more energy you're going to save. Getting the most rideable distance out of the road while using your brakes as little as possible is the payoff for finding the proper line. On a right-hand turn, for example, what this means is going from the far left-hand side of the road, diving into the corner, crossing perpendicular to the apex, as close as possible, and then rolling out to the far left-hand side of the road as you exit the corner. The path should be a nice, gentle arc that will allow for the maximum speed possible.

In a Group

In a race, riders massed across the road and approaching a corner have little choice in the line they are going to take. Any riders too far to the inside are going to be cut off. It's better to be near the middle or outside for a smooth and faster line. The best place to be during a race with a large pack and many corners is sitting right near the front. This way you can choose your own line through the corner. Another important reason to be near the front is that large groups tend to "yo-yo" through corners. The first riders through don't have to brake too much, but the farther back in the pack you are, the more you will have to slow down for the corner. Jumping out of every corner to stay in contact with the leaders wastes much valuable strength.

Lean the Body

As you begin your dive into the corner, lean your body in the direction of the corner. Leaning accomplishes two things.

Photograph 4–4. Setting up your line for a corner is much easier if you are near the front of the pack or don't have riders on either side of you.

First, on high-speed cornering, the way you lean your body is the direction you will steer. The more heavily you lean, the harder you will turn. Second, leaning your body into a corner is the only way you are going to stay up.

The next rule is always to lean your body more than your bike (unless you're not going very fast). If you watch the best racers going through corners, you see that their inside leg is pointed out a bit, and their inside shoulder is a bit lower as they lean their bodies out more than their bikes. This technique lowers the center of gravity of the rider on the bike and makes him more stable through the corner. It's necessary to be very stable so the tires will have good traction on the road.

Braking

Using the brakes properly is also very critical for negotiating a corner at the fastest and safest speed. Always use your front brake more than your rear in cornering. The front brake gives better control and stops you more quickly. (It will also send you over the handlebars if you're not careful.) The front brake also gives a livelier stopping action: the bike seems to spring forward when you release the brake levers.

If you are familiar with the corner before going into it, as should be the case with criteriums, you should be able to judge it so that you do all your braking and slowing down before the apex. If you have to continue to brake after the apex, you've blown it. Either you didn't take the proper line or you didn't slow down properly beforehand. The roll-out after the apex is for reacceleration. There is a tremendous amount of stress placed on the tires when leaning hard in a corner. Adding the force of braking hard increases the possibility of losing traction. The tires will want to slip both sideways and forward.

Rain, Sand, Gravel, and Bumps

Slow down! Wet roads are treacherous. Not only are the roads slippery, but braking action is impaired substantially. Taking the most gentle arc through the corner and keeping the bike as upright as possible will help increase the tire traction and reduce the possibility of slipping out. It's important to know that the road surface is most slick just as it begins to rain due to all the motor oils rising up out of the cracks.

Very experienced racers slow way down just as it begins to rain on a criterium circuit. A few laps later, if the rain keeps up and washes the roads clean, the cyclists will continually increase their speed in the corners, ever so slightly, to find the maximum possible speed. When a racer begins to feel the tires slip, that's it, the limit.

Since most corners are swept clean for criteriums, probably the only time you will run across sand or gravel is during a long road race or when out training. In both of these cases, take it a bit slower since a few lost seconds are not that critical. Sand on top of pavement can be as bad as ice on a road, and gravel is very unpredictable.

A bumpy corner can be equally hazardous; the bike will bounce over the bumps, causing the tires to lose traction with the road. The danger of losing control is compounded if the cyclist happens to have the brakes on through the corner. As the wheel goes airborne for a split second, with its brakes on, it will lock up and stop rolling instantly. When the wheel comes back down to meet the pavement, the tire will be skidding. Never brake hard on a bumpy corner.

Practice

Like just about everything else in cycling, cornering takes practice. A really good way to work on cornering is to find a large, empty parking lot or deserted block to ride laps around. Without any traffic or distractions you can concentrate on all the various aspects of proper cornering. As you gain experience and begin to feel confident in your ability, you might want to increase your speed.

Once you find the maximum safe speed for a particular corner, the only way to make the corner faster is to start your reacceleration out of the corner sooner. Begin the pedal stroke as soon as possible after passing the apex of the corner while you're still leaning the bike, all the while being cautious not to hit a pedal on the pavement. Since different bikes have bottom brackets of different heights, it is essential for you to know the maximum angle that you can lean with your frame before a pedal scrapes the pavement. By placing one of the pedals down and leaning the bike over in that direction, you can stand behind it and check the angle.

A really proficient criterium cyclist is able to pedal out of a hard corner and have his pedal come within a quarter to an eighth inch of the pavement each time. If you feel confident with your ability on the bike, go ahead and hit your pedal a few times (lightly!) so you will know what it feels like and know how to handle it.

The last and most important technical tip on cornering that we have to offer is this: be careful! This does not mean to be so frozen with fear and so carried away with caution that you slow down unnecessarily when entering corners. Bodily rigidity and heavy hands on brakes do more to cause accidents than to prevent them. Being careful doesn't mean closing your eyes and expecting the worst to happen; quite the contrary. It means staying cool, calm, relaxed, and very attentive—attentive to the road conditions, your bike, and the riders all around you. This type of focused awareness coupled with lots of practice can make cornering one of the most successful of your riding skills.

Taking on the Hills

Climbing, sooner or later, becomes the moment of truth for all cyclists. Of course, some riders are natural climbers—they have a light frame and no extra weight, an ideal muscle-to-weight ratio, good cardiovascular fitness, and they relish each climb as a challenge. But many of us dread the hills and, if we have a choice, avoid them, even if it means extra miles to go around the monsters. Still, to be a good cyclist you've got to learn to tackle the climbs. You simply can't avoid them, so instead of trying, why not learn to climb effectively? Losing a few pounds of excess fat will make the process easier, but hard work is also necessary if you are to develop your strength and technique.

Position on the Bike for Climbing

Most pros today, when making time on the ascent, spend a lot of time out of the saddle. However, there are some cyclists noted for sitting and spinning successfully. Therefore, it is important for you to experiment to find out what style works best for you. Most likely you will find yourself sitting in some climbing situations and rising out of the saddle in others.

Let's analyze a typical climb. For a small hill, you start out sitting and spinning in a predetermined gear. As it gets tough and your rpms drop below 85, you stand, being careful not to pull your bike to the rear. You continue this way until you are honking it over the crest. A good rule for beginners is to sit when doing over 85 rpm and to stand when your rpms fall below 85. (Remember to figure your rpms by counting complete revolutions of one foot.)

Long climbs call for a different strategy. Energy needs to be conserved for a sustained, steady effort, so most of the climb should be made in the saddle. When you get tired, you can get out of the saddle for a short time to relieve muscle tension, then sit again. As you alternate between sitting and standing, you may also find it helpful to shift gears. Generally speaking, you can climb in one gear higher out of the saddle than while sitting.

Photograph 4–5. To conserve energy stay in the saddle most of the time during a long climb and adopt the gear and cadence combination you find most efficient.

When standing, your hands should be on the brake hoods for easier breathing. Mentally check to be sure you are pulling up on the pedals, not just pushing down. Keep your center of gravity over the bottom bracket for more power and resist pushing your body forward over the handlebars. Any violent throwing of the bike from side to side or other exaggerated motion should be avoided for maximum efficiency, especially with a loaded bike.

Climbing a long distance in the saddle calls for a lower than normal rpm. The optimum cadence may range from as low as 60 up to about 80 rpm. Adopt the gear and cadence that you find most efficient for the situation. Let your muscles "feel" out the right rpm. While sitting, the top half of your body should be relaxed. Concentrate on breathing from your diaphragm and on using a full pedaling motion. Riding with your hands on the drops in an aerodynamic position at these slow speeds is not necessary. Ride on the tops for better breathing.

If you opt for the higher gear/lower rpm end of the spectrum, you will need to sit back on the saddle and concentrate on your power stroke. A lot of upper body strength must be put into the stroke. Pull back on the bars while pushing forward and down on the pedals, using your weight and upper body strength as efficiently as possible to propel your bike uphill. Some upper body movement is inevitable in this type of powerstroking, but you should avoid wasting energy by thrashing around unnecessarily on your bike. Changing positions on the saddle, forward or back, every kilometer or so on a long climb will work the muscles a bit differently and keep them fresh longer. Also, a frequent change of hand position on the tops of the bars will help keep your arms and shoulders from tiring.

Getting off the seat adds power to the pedal stroke for hard efforts up steep hills, but it also uses more energy. Good technique is important for maximizing the value of that energy. Use your body weight and upper body strength effectively by pulling with your right arm as your right leg pushes down on the power stroke, then shift your weight from right to left and pull on the bars as you push with the left leg. On steep grades, your bike will have a natural sway as you "walk" it up the hill. Just make sure you keep moving in a straight line instead of zigzagging along the road.

Photograph 4–6. When climbing out of the saddle, maximize your energy by shifting your body weight back and forth to put it behind each power stroke.

Gearing—Critical for Efficient Climbing

There is a gear or gearing sequence for each climb. With short hills, the less shifting you do, the better. When encountering an unfamiliar steep climb (a "wall") at a slow pace, out of a turn or switchback, it is easier to shift up than to shift down. Begin a climb like this in a low gear. When going from sitting to standing, since your rpms tend to slow down, shifting up one gear works best to maintain the same speed, providing your gear ratios are not more than one or two teeth apart. Longer climbs mean more shifting as required.

Ideal Climbing Equipment

While it would be wrong to buy a bike solely for hill climbing unless you plan to enter hill climb races, you may be interested to know that a longer crank length can aid by giving better leverage in a big gear. A short wheelbase, with upright frame angles and short rear stays, is helpful for a positive, responsive bike with no wasted effort. (Some hill climbers have used track bikes with fixed gears on shorter climbs in the past.) A low bottom bracket height of about 10½ inches is ideal. This makes the bike easier to control while out of the saddle because the lower center of gravity means less upper body movement and, thus, less fatigue. Cycling shoes with cleats are also a must for any serious climbing.

Climbing Strategy when Riding in a Group

If you always find yourself off the back of the pack after a climb, try to be at the front of the group at the start of each climb. Then if you drift back in the group during the climb, you still have a chance to make up the distance on the descent. Try to evaluate the climb as you approach it. You will want to formulate a plan for covering the hill quickly and efficiently. With a bit of experience you will know when to climb in or out of the saddle (or when to combine these techniques), and you'll know what degree of effort will work best. Since there is no significant draft from other riders, climbing is very much an individual effort. Learn to pace yourself and ride your own tempo.

It is a good idea to train by climbing with someone who climbs well. Sit on your friend's wheel, focus your eyes on the center of his back, and set an identical pace. Before you know it, you will be over the top. If you don't master this at first, just stay with him as long as you can. Your persistence will eventually pay off.

The competitive rider must be aware of some climbing tactics. From a racer who is good on hills, you can expect repeated jumps in an effort to wear down the average riders. If a known climber goes for it, your reaction should be instinctive and without delay to stay with him or her. On a circuit course with a hill, the climber will usually make the pace brutal each time going up, dropping riders on every lap. If you have some climbing ability yourself, a good tactic is to make a move at the start of the climb. Just as other riders are shifting down, you power by them from behind without shifting down until later. They will be caught fumbling for the correct gear.

If you are trying to out-climb somebody else, don't say anything that might bolster your opponent's mental strength. If, for example, you are asked how far it is to the top, don't answer or else say something misleading. With two equally matched riders, the one who can persevere best through the pain will be victorious. To keep yourself going, here's a tip for tourist and racer alike: try singing a song in your mind to the rhythm of the climb and focus your eyes on a point way up in front of you. When you reach it, focus on a new point, and so on to the top.

Photograph 4–7. A racer good at climbing will frequently try to jump away from the other riders on hills to wear them down.

Training for Climbing

You must start at your own level, whether touring or racing, but start you must! Do a climb of from 200 to 800 feet twice a week. Time each climb and incorporate this into your normal riding. If you don't have any climbs, it may help to train by using big gears into the wind, or ride a tandem with someone who is overweight and doesn't want to work hard. If possible, do intervals on a ergometer, a stationary bike, or other high-resistance machine.

New riders not only need to undertake proper training, they also need to establish their proper weight. It's a good idea to keep a daily weight chart. When you do well on climbs, list your weight, along with other factors, on your training calendar for reference. Eventually you'll come up with your ideal weight. If you must lose more than ten pounds, do it in the off-season, or you may just get weaker and risk getting sick.

Tips from a Super-Climber

If you find that you are not a born climber, don't worry about it, advises Giovanni Battaglin, the man acclaimed as the number one climber in Italian pro cycling. Don't spend so much time trying to be good at things for which your body type is ill suited that you neglect the special talents that you do have. Rare indeed is the cyclist who can do everything well. Most of us have to be content with being better at some riding skills than others. So, if you don't climb strongly, find out what you can do well and cultivate that.

The way to get the most out of whatever natural talent you have for climbing, says Battaglin, is to "train in the hills." But don't allow hill work to rob you of time and energy you need to maximize your best riding skills. This precaution aside, here are the highlights of Battaglin's advice on how to approach climbing in training and racing.

1. In early season training, avoid all hills until you have accumulated 1,200 to 1,500 miles. During the next 500 to 800 miles, begin riding in rolling terrain and gradually increase the length and steepness of the climbs. After 2,000 miles you should be ready for hills of any length.

2. If you live where there is no flat area at all, use a very low gear so you can spin up the hills easily during the first 1,500 miles. Even so, do not ride any hills of 5 miles or longer.

3. A technique when first starting to train on a hill is to ride up easily until the last quarter mile, then go harder. The next time, go harder the last half mile, then the last three quarters of a mile. Hill training must be worked into—don't start off by jamming up the entire distance.

4. Someone who has the physical attributes for climbing— light body and slender muscles—will gain the most from training on hills. The percentage of his or her improvement in climbing will be significantly greater than that of someone who does not have these physical characteristics.

5. It is never correct to climb with hands on the drops of the handlebars. Doing so upsets your weight distribution on the bike and hinders deep breathing. Use an upright position with hands on the tops or brake levers. This is also easier on your back.

6. Moderation is the key to handling the bike on a climb. When standing, don't throw the bike excessively to the side; likewise, don't try to keep it stiffly upright. Be in balance and do not exaggerate either way.

7. Whether training or racing, always start a climb as slowly as possible and then increase the pace. You must accustom your body to the breathing and rhythm of the climb before the hard effort can start.

8. All early season climbing should be devoted to developing a rhythm. This climbing should always be a steady effort, never with jumps. You must synchronize the body rhythm and the breathing rhythm with the pedal rhythm.

9. Anytime you are able to spin up a hill, do so. If you push a big gear, there is a greater chance of blowing up in the second half and losing considerable time. If you are already pushing when the attacks come, your legs will be tight, and you won't be able to respond.

10. Always try to arrive at the foot of the hill among the first 10 to 12 riders. If you are near the back, you can be sure of spending twice the energy to stay in contact because a guy ahead of you will miss a shift or start weaving, creating a gap. The group might begin to split, and you won't be able to do anything about it even if you see it happen.

11. A climbing specialist will spend equal time on and off the saddle. A pacer or sprinter who is not a natural climber will sit most of the time and push a higher gear. Francesco Moser, for example, usually sits and powers his way up. Eddy Merckx used to drop people simply by imposing his pace, doing 90 percent of a climb sitting down. The light, skinny, natural climbers, on the other hand, do a lot of their work off the saddle.

12. If possible, try to stay in a slightly lower gear than the guy in front of you. This will help you stay looser and more supple than he is.

13. To attack on a hill, go into a higher gear so you can open a significant gap, then return to an easier gear. The climbing specialist will shift many times on a hill, but the pacer tends to stay in a gear that gives him the rhythm he likes. He won't shift much unless changes in the grade of the road force him to.

14. The best way to attack is to get at the back of the group, let a five-yard gap open, then jump on it. By the time you pass the group, you will have a big edge in speed, and you may be able to gain 30 to 40 yards before they can respond. This technique is also valid for attacking on the flats—jumping from the back is always better than from the front.

15. A good time to attack is when an opponent is using his water bottle or shifting gears. In either case he has to finish what he is doing before he can begin to chase, and by then you will have a good gap. The idea is to cause your opponent to expend more energy closing the gap than you expended opening it.

16. Heavier riders should not try to keep up with the pure climbers. If they are going at a speed you can handle, ride with them, but if they start jumping with two or three miles remaining to the top, let them go and keep your own pace.

17. Should you feel that you are blowing up on the climb, slow down. You can lose ten minutes if you keep pushing until you go to pieces, but you might lose only three or four minutes if you reduce your pace. If you go up slowly and throw your weight on the pedals, you can make any climb without blowing up.

18. If you have been able to stay with the leaders into the final mile of the climb and then the pace really gets moving, make a supreme effort to get to the top with them. You may succeed and then you can rest on the descent. If you can't quite stay up, you will still be close enough to catch them.

19. Always try to crest a climb with enough strength left so that your reflexes aren't shot. This is important for fast but safe descending—you must have the mental clarity to choose the correct line through curves. Otherwise, you could lose all the time you worked so hard for on the way up.

Practicing techniques such as these is not only a good way to develop the physical strength and endurance you need to be a good climber, it also has tremendous psychological value. The terror of hills is largely mental, a combination of dreading the pain you expect to experience and fearing that you cannot make it to the top or will arrive there too exhausted to resume riding at a normal pace. By training in the manner suggested, you can make the hills much less awesome. Instead of monsters to be avoided at all costs, they will become simply testing grounds for your newly acquired balance of physical strength and technical mastery.

Credits

The information in this book is drawn from these and other articles from *Bicycling* magazine.

"Basic Riding Techniques Worth Mastering" Thomas Prehn, "Back to the Basics," *Bicycling*, March 1983, pp. 22–27.

"Riding the Paceline" Thomas Prehn, "Honor Among Cyclists," *Bicycling*, June 1982, pp. 34–36.

"Reading the Road" Thom Lieb, "Reading the Road," *Bicycling*, April 1982, pp. 16–19; John S. Allen, "Emergency Turning and Braking," *Bicycling*, January/February 1982, pp. 27–33.

"Save the Wheels" Thomas Prehn, "Save the Wheels," *Bicycling*, April 1983, p. 23.

"Riding Fast in the City"   John S. Allen, "Riding Fast in the City," *Bicycling*, May 1982, pp. 44–48.

"Taking Your Place on the Road"   John S. Allen, "Assertive Cycling," *Bicycling*, July 1982, pp. 59–63.

"Any Cyclist Can Benefit from Riding Racer-Smooth" Thomas Prehn, "Any Cyclist Can Benefit from Riding Racer-Smooth," *Bicycling*, April 1982, p. 42.

"Improve Your Technique with Fixed-Gear Training" Tom Petrie, "Greet the New Season with Fixed Gear Training," *Bicycling*, March 1981, pp. 109–13.

"Learn to Read a Race and Let Conditions Determine Tactics"   Thomas Prehn, "Reading a Race," *Bicycling*, September/October 1984, pp. 34–36.

"Descending—Fast and Safely"   Thomas Prehn, "Descending—Getting Radical," *Bicycling*, September/October 1982, pp. 28–30.

"Cornering for Racers"   Thomas Prehn, "Cornering for Racers," *Bicycling*, July 1982, pp. 54–57.   ·

"Taking on the Hills"   Curt Bond, "Taking the Hell Out of Hills," *Bicycling*, July 1981, pp. 34–36; Thomas Prehn, "Climbing Efficiently," *Bicycling*, August 1982, pp. 45–49; Ed Pavelka, "Making it to the Top," *Bicycling*, September/October 1984, pp. 52–61.

Photos and Illustrations

Angelo Caggiano: photos 1–6, 2–1, and 2–2; Carl Doney: photo 3–2; Susan Eastman: photos 4–5 and 4–6; Robert F. George: photo 1–7; Bob Gerheart: photos 1–1, 1–8, and 3–3; T. L. Gettings: photos 1–2, 3–4, 3–5, and 4–3; Anthony Rodale: photo 1–4; Christie C. Tito: photo 1–5; Sally Shenk Ullman: photos 1–3, 1–9, 2–3, 2–4, 2–5, 2–6, 2–7, 2–8, 3–1, 4–2, 4–4, and 4–7; Bonnie Wong: photo 4–1. George Retseck: all illustrations.